Kelly's book immediately gripped
to share her lived experiences is pai
of protecting her readers from vicari

story
beautifully with post-exit healing and reflection, a key piece that is
needed to be heard by survivors in the process of their own journeys
to freedom. Kelly's voice is an important one in the anti-trafficking
and trauma survivor communities.

MEGAN LUNDSTROM
EXECUTIVE DIRECTOR, FREE OUR GIRLS

Life for Kelly Patterson, my friend and colleague, was virtually hell
on earth. In vulnerable and vivid language, Kelly recounts her days
trafficked for sex. It is our duty to comprehend the frightful world of
these victims so that we join God in rescuing them. This is Kelly's
reason for writing. This is also the story of the enormous work
required to wait and maintain a belief that God will eventually come
to one's rescue, and Kelly's very life will assure every reader that the
waiting and believing is worth it all.

SCOTT W. CRAIG
ANTI-TRAFFICKING ADVOCATE
LANDMARK COMMUNITY CHURCH PASTOR
FORMER SOUTH DAKOTA STATE CONGRESSMAN

In her book *From Trafficked to Treasured*, Kelly does an amazing
job of helping the reader understand more about the horrifying
realities of trafficking without giving unnecessary, graphic details
that could make the book difficult to read. She also explains
complicated topics like dissociation in ways that takes away the

mystery. This brings helpful clarity to both survivors of trauma as well as those who want to be better equipped to come alongside them in a meaningful way. Kelly shares her story and insights with honesty and courage. Her sincerity and authenticity will surely help other survivors of sexual abuse make sense of their own experiences, so they can continue moving forward toward the fullness of life.

I highly recommend *From Trafficked to Treasured* to survivors of trafficking as well as to those working with survivors of trafficking and trauma.

DENI ANDERSON
FOUNDER OF JUSTICE PLUS FREEDOM
REBECCA BENDER INITIATIVE LIFE COACH

I read it twice! It's that good! This is an amazing, hard-to-put down book that is very timely for today! Kelly does an incredible job in exposing the horrific issues of sex-trafficking as well as bringing hope for healing for anyone who has been touched by this life-altering crime. It's an eye-opener but not a downer. Read and be inspired to do more to bring the darkness to light and reach those who are still trapped.

AMAZON CUSTOMER

From Trafficked To Treasured

Kelly R Patterson

Published by
Red Door Sentinel
Rapid City, South Dakota
www.reddoorsentinel.com

Paperback ISBN: 978-0-9980909-3-1

Cover and graphics by JewelDesign
Author photo by How Eye See It Photography

Revision 2

I dedicate this book to my survivor brothers and sisters around the world, to those who are free, and to those still in captivity. You are wounded soldiers and heroes of a war you never enlisted for.

TABLE OF CONTENTS

FOREWORD

The Lord often reveals things to me about my mother while I am in the middle of praying or worshipping and when she is far from my thoughts. It occurs during times when I am unaware of any hardships that she is going through. I believe the Lord does this so there is no doubt that what He is revealing in that moment is from Him. It always floods over me instantly, with an overwhelming amount of emotion that usually brings me to tears.

My mother has always been protective about letting me know too many details about her past concerning the trauma she has been through. She always puts everyone before herself, so I rarely knew when my mother was dealing with something difficult. I still do not know many details of my mother's past, and we keep it that way, as we know her suffering can be too much for a daughter to hear. Even though I am an adult, she continues to protect me.

The first time God spoke to me about my mother's hardships that are recorded in this book, He began to show me all the trauma that my mother had been through in flashes of pictures. This was before I knew anything about it. He said to me, "Think of all of the things you have suffered in your life. Your mother has suffered those as well, but far more and much worse." As soon as the Lord revealed each memory of my own difficulties and the comparison of what my mother had been through, I fell to my knees and began to cry. The pain I felt through my own experiences were hard enough! I could not imagine living through the things my mother has been through! God was not devaluing my past sufferings, instead He was revealing how incredible it was that she was not only surviving all of this but thriving in life as well as using her suffering to help others.

I would soon find out these revelations were happening the same time my mother was coping with the pain of reliving her past through horrific flashbacks and memories. It was one of the hardest times in her life.

With all that my mother has been through, she could have become a bitter, angry person, and yet she is far from that. Many who have had the life she has had end up on the streets or an abandoned building with a needle in their arm trying to numb the pain. I do not mean that in a derogatory way for people living in those situations; in fact, I understand that with a significant amount of suffering in someone's life, it can often feel like too much to bear and can be extremely difficult to cope with. Yet, my mother is not only dealing with all of the pain but is also reaching out to others and helping them.

You see, during this time the Lord was showing me what an incredible and rare beauty my mother is. It is difficult to find someone who has suffered so much and is still such a beautiful person inside and out! It is even more difficult to find someone who is willing to use all their pain and suffering to glorify the Lord and to help and love others. That is the kind of life that can only come from the hope and healing that happens through a relationship with Jesus. If you met my mother, you would never guess she has suffered so much. In fact, most people are shocked to learn of her past. I am extremely honored knowing someone who is so selfless, and I am even more blessed that she is my mother.

A couple of years after this first experience, the Lord began to show me the amount of love and admiration He has for my mom. It came to me in a series of short bursts that lasted for a few minutes every day for about a week. It would flood over me in an overwhelming and all-consuming moment filled with love and admiration of how wonderful my mother is. This is a love that cannot be explained in worldly terms. All I knew was that I could only handle so much at one time, and that is why it lasted only a few minutes. God not only showed me how much He loves my mom, but He also allowed me to see her through His eyes.

I wanted to share this experience with my mother, but all I could tell her was how He looked at her with a smile on His face, and how proud He is of her. Once again, because of her protectiveness, I was completely unaware that during this time, my mother was struggling with even more memories and questioning how the Lord could ever be proud of her knowing her past. I can tell you this; He treasures her more than she will ever know in this life! No matter how she feels about her past, or how it looks to the world around her, the Lord sees none of it in the same way we do.

Foreword

To the survivors reading this, know that it is no coincidence that you picked up this book. I guarantee that no matter how you feel, God sees you the same way He sees my mother. It is my prayer that you will be given hope and healing through her story and be able to begin to comprehend just how much the Lord also treasures you.

Jessica
Kelly's daughter

ACKNOWLEDGEMENTS

To my husband, David, who is my very best friend, thank you for your endless love and your tireless dedication to helping me be all that I can be in this life. It would take an entire book to say all that I wish to say about your selflessness, your integrity, your kindness, your love, and your incredible character. Your love has truly saved me.

To my children, grandchildren, and other family members, I am so grateful for your support and care. You are my cheerleading squad and you have held me up when I needed extra support. Thank you for affirming me in this endeavor. I love you more than words can express.

Thank you to my editors and proofreaders, Judy Mildren, Dawn Pence, and Gina Dvorak. Where would this book be without

Acknowledgements

your devotion to excellence and your tireless efforts to walk through this journey with me? While you endured shedding tears over these pages, you remained persistent to help me finish.

Kelly Whitaker, as my publisher, and my friend, you have taught me so much and have challenged me to have a devotion to detail. I can scarcely thank you enough. Thank you for giving me the opportunity to put this all on paper and get it out there for others.

A special thank you to those who are my dear friends and church family for supporting me in such a daring undertaking. You not only support my efforts, but you pray faithfully for me at every turn. You have walked much of this out with me. You are a loving and irreplaceable people.

Lastly, but most importantly, I thank the Creator for walking me through this long venture. More than that, thank You for caring so much for me and for showing me that I have purpose.

From
Trafficked
To
Treasured

INTRODUCTION

My name "Kelly" means brave. Writing this book feels like the most courageous thing I have ever done. In the process of putting words to paper, flashbacks of unwanted memories would cause me to rehash extremely painful events. Facing the potential that some people may think differently of me or not understand me due to what is written in these pages had to be reconciled as a risk I am willing to take. Considering how it may affect my husband and family also weighs on my heart.

However, the cry of the voiceless ones that are still trapped in sex slavery won out! Staying silent is not an option for me while so many are still living the life that I once did. If this book changes a heart, frees a soul, or heals a body, it will far outweigh any pain it took to create it.

Introduction

While each survivor's experiences are different, they are also very much the same. Some things are so similar that another survivor reading this will feel as though they are reading their own story. It is my hope that through my experiences, I will help expose a much underrated and underestimated issue in the USA with ring trafficking in its Heartland (Midwest).

To all who personally knew me in my younger years—you most likely were never aware of what was happening in my secret life. There will be many possible reactions to learning about the behind-the-scene incidents. You may feel guilt because you did not notice; you may feel like it cannot be possible; you may be confused; you may be shocked; and/or you may feel that it makes sense and fills in some blanks. It was what it was. More importantly, it is no more!

There may be some triggering events shared within the pages of this book. It is a very fine line to write about the topic of sex trafficking and avoid being too explicit or graphic. I worked extremely hard to find the balance of giving enough information without giving too much.

If you have sexual abuse in your background, while difficult to face, please keep in mind that I wrote this especially for you! It is my deepest desire that my life's journey will aid you in moving forward, wherever you are stuck or wherever you are in your journey. It is my hope that you will be comforted, blessed, and receive insights that will promote you to be more than a survivor!

I hope that it will educate those who are unaware of the tragic nature of sex trafficking and how truly life altering it is—to call you to action, compassion, and understanding. Additionally, this book is for all the family and friends of survivors. I pray that this will help you walk it out with your loved ones and have the patience and love needed to be there for them.

Introduction

My personal beliefs include the existence of a sovereign God who loves me. He was not happy about the things that happened to me. However, God did not hide His face from it either. He was present. That knowledge alone will trigger many readers, just as that knowledge triggered me to ask the tough questions.

Walking and wrestling with my feelings towards God was a long journey regarding what has happened to me. I would expect nothing less from any survivor. You do not need to believe as I do to gain greater healing, empowerment, enlightenment, education, and understanding from reading about my journey. I landed where I am with my beliefs in God through much struggling, searching other religions, feeling anger toward God, being afraid of God, ignoring God, and finally receiving healing from the God of all Creation.

There is no way to gently begin unfolding the horrific things that my mind and body endured. However, my journey will offer hope, education, and understanding of the hidden issues between the painful details. While this book will flow somewhat chronologically, it will more so intentionally tackle this topic with the emphasis on the many complex issues surrounding trafficking. Much like a movie that draws you in and out of the present, the contents of this book will occasionally digress or progress in time and then strategically bring you back into the present to hit the specific issues.

This book is not only about my journey of survival with trauma but includes woven stories of the unique ways that a very intimate God ministers to those in great pain. It also contains accounts of God's supernatural moments in my life. He is the same God today as He was for Esther, Moses, Joseph, Tamar, and Rahab. God has not changed! (Be sure to use the glossary at the end of the book for terms you do not understand.)

Sincerely, Kelly

BROKEN BUT NOT DESTROYED

When I accidentally broke a lovely piece of pottery recently, I was reminded of King David's lament in Psalms 31:12, "I am forgotten as though I were dead; I have become like broken pottery."

Have you ever felt like this broken piece of pottery? Do you feel as David did? Broken and forgotten? Are you afraid to express how you feel?

I have felt broken and forgotten many times in my life. Some of those periods lasted for years, some much shorter. When any person suffers long-term, ongoing abuse, it is quite likely you will identify with this piece of pottery and with me. As we begin to unearth the hidden things associated with sex trafficking, I believe you will easily identify why a person would feel so shattered and irreparable. When pottery shatters, it cannot be restored. You can glue it together, but all the cracks will show. I am grateful that we are not restored that way. Our Creator works wonders!

David's expression of the state of his soul was not an expression of lack of faith. His responses are an example to us that we can speak honestly to God about our emotions and come to Him in our pain.

Just two verses later in Psalms 31:14, David says, "But I trust in you, Lord; I say, 'You are my God.'" God wants our honesty. It is there, in our shattered state, that He can begin to pick up the pieces. Not only can God restore us from our broken state, He also upgrades us to a better version of pottery than we were before our brokenness.

I have a passion. I work with human trafficking, ritual abuse, sexual abuse, and sexual assault survivors. It is my great privilege to be allowed to sit with survivors and observe as the Lord heals them and to see them walk out their freedom from lies, shame, betrayal, anger, terror, etc. Why do I have this passion? Because I am one of them.

For me, the initial sexual abuse began at age four-years old by someone close to our family. My understanding of personal boundaries was lost at a very early age due to multiple sexual predators. I did not understand the most basic boundary—my own skin, my own body. I had been threatened not to tell or else. Whatever the "or else" was, I was afraid enough to not find out. Additionally, I did not even know what to call what was happening to me. I had no education regarding this. There were no words. It was unspeakable and undefinable.

My family moved every few years to different communities in and out of our state due to my Dad's occupation. These moves did not stop what was happening to me. I had no understanding that I was being groomed by an organized ring. By the age of nine years old, I was being photographed for underground explicit porn magazines.

Gang rapes became the way to control me and break me down completely. The final breaking of any form of control over what happened to my own body resulted from my first gang rape at age thirteen. This was initially done by a snatch and grab where I was stalked and pulled into a vehicle when I least expected it, and by people I never suspected would take things so far. They took me to their home and drove directly into the garage. As they pulled me out of the car, they all began ripping my clothing off. I was in shock! Horrified! I knew one of them and the idea of him seeing me this way added extra humiliation to the situation. Things became very serious when they threw me against the wall and nearly knocked me out because I was fighting back. As I was then thrown to the ground, they held a knife between my legs and told me not to move. I was savagely raped by each of them.

They then drug me into the house, where they spent the rest of the day taking turns repeatedly raping and abusing me. Somewhere in the middle of this incident, they took out a scalpel and three of them each carved a long line into my back. I felt the hot burning pain of the cuts and the blood running down my back. The others had to stop one of the guys, because he was cutting too deep. They then turned me over and carved three lines into my right wrist. These monsters marked me, so I would never forget who I belonged to.

Some of what is done in these situations is simply insane. They literally took a "break" to watch football and made me sit with them. Our bathroom at home had a window in it so I assumed that theirs would also. Seeing this as a possible escape route, I said that I needed to go to the bathroom. Once inside the bathroom door, I locked it with the mistaken idea that I was about to get free. At this point, much to my horror, the realization that there was no window hit me! I stayed in there and washed up, cried, trying to catch my breath, and finally sat down in utter disbelief that I was trapped. Eventually they came knocking and telling me I had nowhere to run. I just kept the door locked and hoped. Unfortunately, it was no big effort for them to break the door down and force me back to the bedroom where they tied me down to the bed and continued their savagery.

My heart sank at the desperation of my situation, until I finally just tried to go blank: to not feel, to not see, to not hear, to not be. Of course, they would not allow me to stay that way. They intentionally did all they could to bring me into it with them, to force me to be present.

The devastation of forcing the physical feeling of pleasure on you during extreme terror and fear of death is another way of breaking a person down. It produces shame and guilt mixed with confusion. The ambivalence is difficult to overcome and requires much ongoing healing. Nearly anyone who has suffered long term ongoing sexual abuse or sex trafficking has had to deal with this issue.

The memory of being dropped off down the alley from my home has always stayed with me. I no longer felt like me. The world felt different. As I walked the longest short distance of my life, I began to come up with a story. I had to explain all the bruises and blood, my torn clothing, my broken glasses. What would I say? As I entered the back yard, I saw my bicycle lying on the grass. It was then that I came up with my cover story. I had a bicycle wreck. I rehearsed the story over and over until I believed it myself. In an attempt to add further evidence to my story, I picked up my bike and threw it down a couple times so that it could look a little damaged. I looked at the handle bar, and bizarre as it is, I came up with another cover story for my mother.

Upon entering our house bloody and bruised, I told Mom about the "bike wreck." I told her I just wanted to soak in the tub. She asked if I needed help and I told her I was okay. I then turned and asked her a strange question, one she would always wonder about.

I asked, "Mom, could I lose my virginity if the bicycle handle hit me hard between the legs?" She commented something to the effect that she guessed it was possible. I went on my way, soaking all my pain and memory away in a bathtub full of forgetfulness.

Mom told me that she had always remembered this day and years later wondered why she had not questioned me further. Even the idea of being raped was an unheard-of notion for the small town of America that we lived in. This sort of thing just does not happen there. Why would she ask further? Additionally, I was an extremely honest child. She had no reason to doubt my word.

I was gang raped again in this community by a much larger group of guys. I was supposed to be spending the weekend with a friend. When I arrived at her house, her brother told me that she was not home and that he would take me to her. Since I knew him, I thought nothing of it and took the ride to where I thought she was. Meanwhile, he gave me a Coke that was laced with Spanish Fly, an incredibly dangerous drug that could have killed me. It initially caused me to be violently ill, along with being very high.

I was hung by my hands from the rafters in a barn outside of town. Then began the longest weekend of my life up to that point. They were charging a fee at the door to be a part of this. Another girl had been brought in and tied up in the same way. She was released when her brother arrived on the scene. Meanwhile, I was left alone the entire weekend with this brutal group of guys. I learned that there is a dynamic that occurs in gang rapes, a competition of sorts. This is a horrifying thing to experience in about every way imaginable. I felt certain I would die this day. I felt the weekend would never end. Every moment the repeated thought in my mind was, "Please, can this be over now, please?" I could not focus on anything else but that thought. I needed this to be done!

Back then I had heard a phrase that "only sluts get gang banged." I do not know where I heard it, but it was stuck in my mind. Therefore, I determined that as soon as it was over—that it never happened! I rehearsed this in my head, "It never happened."

A few days later, I was approached on a community street by two boys my age, and they asked me, "Did you really do that with all those guys?"

I asked, "Do what?"

They replied, "We didn't think so, never mind." That was that. Nothing happened.

I lost the ability to sleep at night if my parents were out late. My nights were tormented with rape nightmares and my daytime with shame and fear. I literally encircled myself with all my stuffed animals and slept in a fetal position for years. My abuse was blocked, locked away in hazy memories; shadows that haunted me in my nightmares and played out in my teenage life in the form of rebellion.

I had a miscarriage after that first gang rape. In the forefront of my mind has always been the memory of the horrific pain I endured for several days—so painful that it would drop me to the ground. I remember the day I miscarried very clearly, as the pain was so severe that I literally crawled on my hands and knees for half a block to my house.

At this stage of my life, I was new to womanhood and I did not understand that the large "mass" that I passed was not normal. When I described it to my mother at the time, she was very alarmed and told me if that ever happened again to let her inspect it. She was assuming it may have been something normal, but still showed concern. Mom did not have a clue. Neither did I. After all, I had no conscious memory of the gang rape by this time, so of course, I believed I was a virgin. Later in life, I named this little baby, "Lyle." My heart felt that I had miscarried a little boy.

I pray for anyone reading this who has lost a child. I pray that they will find their way to peace that only You can give, Lord. Please be close to each one and as You hold their tears in your bottle, remember them in a most compassionate way this very day. Give them hope for the day when they will be reunited with their little one(s)!

CRASHING

I have heard people say that sexual assault victims are asking to be violated. However, one cannot reason that a four-year-old child is being seductive or has a desire to intentionally attract predators. Instead, it is clear that this child has been targeted by someone with a twisted thought process or skewed morals. Yet, that is exactly the age when I was first perpetrated by a grown man. This person was someone close to our family. He was not mean *initially*. He did his best to make me feel *special*. It literally makes me ill to write that, but that is the truth.

By now, you are probably wondering what was missing in my childhood that things could go to the extent they did. You are possibly questioning my family, perhaps my parents in particular. I want to address this from several perspectives. First, never assume any little child at such an impressionable age, no matter how loved, could avoid such a set up. It can happen to anyone and it does.

Was my family life perfect? Of course not. We had problems, some bigger than other families and some much smaller. As a very young child, my parents had their difficulties in marriage as many do. They also enjoyed hanging out at the local bars and partying with friends. We lived in small communities in a sparsely populated state at a time when people felt their children were safe nearly anywhere. There were no Amber Alerts, no discussion of good touch vs bad touch; nobody discussed sexual abuse or rape, let alone trafficking. While we boast about the clean living and safe environment of rural America, there exists a seedy underbelly that is thriving. In the Midwest, other adults were commonly automatically trusted, and children were allowed to run the streets without supervision.

Our family did, however, have something very uncommon compared to others. When I was in fifth grade, my dad was in a near-fatal plane crash. It was a small plane. He and a good friend were the only two occupants in the small plane. Carbon monoxide had been silently leaking into the cockpit undetected, causing them both to eventually pass out. Meanwhile, at the pilot's home, our families were awaiting their return. We were to have a meal together and they were extremely late. The pilot's wife put out a call over Citizen Band (CB) radio asking people to keep an eye out or let them know if they heard any concerning sounds. These were all farmers and ranchers and the CB radio was one way of staying in touch and looking out for one another. It was not very long before quite a bit of disturbing chatter began to come across the radio.

I remember sitting with the son of the pilot listening in terror to CB conversations of people mentioning hearing what they assumed was a plane going down. A pilot then said he sighted what appeared to be a downed plane. Our mothers left immediately for the area where it was spotted. They left the two of us in charge of the younger children so that they were able to go to what was believed to be the general area of the wreckage. He and I sat there, mostly silent, terrified, listening to all the local farmers and ranchers talking over the radio. We then heard the news that their plane had indeed gone down, and that it did not look survivable. I remember the terror, the butterflies in my stomach. We were frozen in time, just sitting, waiting, trying to comfort one another and hoping for the best.

My dad's crashed Cessna airplane

We were later informed that a former pastor discovered the wreckage from his plane. He noticed a white hanky waving out of the remains of the plane. The pilot was alert and waving frantically! It was revealed that the plane went into a nose-dive and spun out of control into the ground. While it appeared that no one could have survived that crash, the plane had come down and impacted in a very large patch of snow. Obviously, it was not their time to permanently enter into eternity!

My dad had lost so much blood that the doctor later told him "there was not even enough blood left in him to touch the dipstick." Dad clinically died that day for several minutes, during which he had a near-death experience.

During the moments he was dead, dad was standing outside in a huge beautiful open area, almost like floating there and wanting to get over to be with the other moving images or beings that he could see. There was a glorious being standing in front of him while dad was longing to get through to the beautiful blue he saw in front of him. He said he could feel a freedom and lightness as though there was no gravity or weight. Something indescribable was coming from over there. However, this beautiful being told him, "no, not yet, it's not your time, Harry."

Dad said he wept bitterly at that moment, and the glorious being repeated the statement, "no, not yet, it's not your time, Harry." Again, dad wept bitterly, but this time he was instantly sent back into his body. Incidentally, to this day, he longs for the day when he can meet the Source of that great freedom and beauty that he had experienced.

My dad remained in a coma for ten days. When he opened his eyes, it was discovered that he had severe traumatic brain injury. In his mind, he was still a teenager when he awoke. Therefore, he recognized my mother because they had dated in high school but could not understand why she looked older. He had to be re-introduced to his children because he did not know us. We were soon to find out that we did not know him anymore either.

The next three years were very difficult. We would frequently awaken to hear dad screaming and crying in pain during the night with horrendous headaches. We were all robbed of peace and of sleep. My dad's behavior was truly like a teenager, and my mother was in her 30's. It was a terrible time in their marriage and very hard on us all.

In God's mercy, the man who spotted the wreckage from his plane returned to ministry. He started a church in our community shortly after the plane crash. He and others invited my family to church several times. It took my dad nearly three years to agree to attend, after feeling he owed it to this Pastor. That very first Sunday, my dad committed his life to God and nearly in that same instant, most of his mind returned to normal. This began a normalcy and a peace in our home that had been missing.

Unfortunately, I was too damaged to join the normalcy of our family at this point. They grew in God and in unity together but without me. Instead, I found isolation was vital to reinforcing the secrets stored within the citadels of denial. I was crashing too, just not in an airplane!

It was during my father's amnesia that those first gang rapes occurred. I was not about to add to my family's issues with my own trauma, so I kept silent. While I had endured previous abuses, the shame and violence of gang rapes caused a total crash of my perceived self-worth, identity, and security.

After all I had been through, a reprieve was needed in my life. I desperately needed a long-term rest. This came about through an unexpected and miserable beginning. I had always been popular in school. My closest friends were the "in" crowd. After the summer of being gang raped the first time, I then entered eighth grade. The first half of the year started out normal as far as school and friendships appeared from outside perspectives, though I endured two more gang rapes during this first semester.

Since some of the same people were tied to all of these rapes, I can only assume these horrific ordeals were intentionally prearranged. The first one seemed to be the result of having been stalked for months by one of the rapists when they took me to their home. The second one was perfectly arranged around a weekend that I was to be spending with a friend. These were the events which I also shared about in the chapter titled, "Broken, but not Destroyed." Unfortunately, the drugs they forced on me did not help me permanently forget these incidents.

The third gang rape was on a snowy day when I was grabbed by some of the same guys, right off the street and drug into a car. They drove me to a graveyard and raped me in the snow on top of a gravestone where they also performed bizarre rituals. Then they left me there alone, naked and tied to an upright grave stone for some time before coming back to release me to walk home in the snow.

Sadly, towards spring, rumors had begun to spread. While I was in denial about the rapes, there was no stopping the continuing ordeal. It spun horribly out of control! I was bullied by nearly the entire middle school. Not only did they make fun of me, call me names, pick on me, and reject me; they also made a pornographic cartooned book about me and passed it around. It was so outrightly horrific that even my bus driver was protecting me daily while I was riding the bus. The principal called me in to her office to ask why all of this was happening to me. I had no answers for her. I had no answers for myself.

I was left with only a handful of student friends who were also being shunned by others. Those beautiful people stood with me through it all and I will never forget them for that. Since that time, I have received sincere apologies from two of my previous classmates who became Christians. The bullying was so horrid that it haunted them for years as well. The apologies validated my pain from the bullying and were greatly appreciated. However, the awful truth of what was happening behind the scenes was not disclosed.

My parents made the decision for dad to take another job position and move away from this community to a Native American reservation. This move gave me the brief reprieve that I needed. I have thanked my parents more than once for making this move, but it is unlikely that anyone can fully understand how badly I needed to relocate! I was never once sexually abused on the reservation. The reservation was my haven and to this day, any reservation I visit is a place that I can sleep for days in such peace. My body remembers.

The move was most likely not as restful for my parents, however, because I was a serious mess! I was always going from one problem to another: drinking heavily, getting in trouble in school, and attempting to run away. It must have been a challenging time for my family trying to live with all the phone calls from teachers and concerned parents regarding my behavior. With the experience of being bullied in the previous community, I moved here with the resolve to never allow myself to fall into the category of not being "cool" again! I was determined to do and become whatever it took to be accepted. The rejection of being bullied nearly killed me inside. In all honesty, I could not emotionally survive that kind of bullying again.

I honor my parents for their willingness to give up their friends and their life to save mine. Since I was getting into so much trouble, they ended up placing me in a boarding school in my junior year. This was yet another sacrifice on their part, especially financially. They were laying down their needs to save their daughter from destruction YET AGAIN and did it willingly without having any knowledge of what was behind my behavior.

That first year in boarding school, I learned so much about God, about the Bible, and about other people. Living in such close quarters with others was actually very good for me. While attending that school, I was very safe, which provided me more reprieve. Without these times of rest both on the reservation and in the boarding school, I am not sure my body could have survived the years of trafficking that were ahead.

For those who are targeted, instincts are not trusted. They often put themselves in dangerous situations. This was true in my case as I began to try to blunt my memories and my pain with drugs and alcohol. I was hanging out with rough crowds. I would drink to the point of blacking out and I would use heavy drugs to "leave" reality. Unfortunately, all of this simply added to my abuse. It is self-destructive behavior that you cannot even make sense of yourself.

Please notice the flow of events here: I was NOT an alcohol and drug user first! That is not what got me into trouble. I used them AFTER my body had been used and defiled by others! There are far too many agencies blaming addictions for the reason people end up being trafficked. It is my belief and my experience that addictions among sex trafficking victims often occur out of the need to escape something that has already happened, or out of the fact that the drugs have been forced upon them and not the other way around.

My use of these substances always made me feel horrendous shame. While shame compelled me to use them, the shame remained and even gained momentum like a never-ending cycle. I am uncertain why my body never became addicted like so many others, but it certainly was not because I had a better handle on life! I could never understand why I felt like the black sheep of our family or what was wrong with me. This feeling compounded the shame I carried from being abused.

Crashing

Being targeted makes you feel like there is something wrong with you. It is only with a great amount of work on my healing journey that I was able to give my back hand to this shame and send it packing. It is not mine to carry. Shame on them!

I pray for more empathy and compassion to come from the public and the Judicial System. I ask for eyes to see the human beings trapped behind the misnomers tied to the Commercial Sex Trafficking industry. May God impart to each one the ability to show compassion to those whom you do not understand.

SEVENTEEN

I was attending the private Christian boarding school my junior year and planned to return to finish out my senior year. Believing that as a Christian, I was safe from all harm and that nothing bad would ever happen to me again, I felt invincible. At the age of 17, my family moved to another state for the summer for missionary training, directly following my own personal decision to follow Christ. We lived on a lake and we spent the summer in the water. It was to be a restful and peaceful summer for us.

One sunny day, I was innocently hanging out near a remote part of the beach on one of the lakes with a boyfriend, when we were suddenly surrounded by a notorious motorcycle gang. These were one percenter bikers. The term, "One Percenter Motorcycle Club" or "One Percenter Bike Gang," is used to describe outlaw motorcycle clubs. This gang circled us a few times, revving their engines and drinking. We were tanning on a blanket in the center. My boyfriend told me to lay very still. I could feel my heart pounding so hard, I thought I would pass out. His was pounding just as hard. He told me to just keep looking in his eyes. I did just that, hoping that by ignoring them, they would just leave. I only have small pieces of this memory.

I remember their leather jackets and the emblems on the back. Unfortunately, I remember the leader's hair color and face. It was the face of a nameless person who would haunt my nightmares throughout my life. Obviously, the trauma was too much, and I fully dissociated from this event. I emotionally left the situation by standing outside of myself, as though watching this happen to someone else. I then blocked out as much as I was able to; and over time it faded into my subconscious. What I do remember today is too graphic to describe. The guy I came with was tied to a tree and helpless. I remember begging him not to tell my parents. However, when that thought would arise in my conscious mind, I could never quite remember what it was I did not want him to tell my parents.

Was this event put into motion by the trafficking ring? It may have been random, as it was several states away from my home state. Yet, I also know that the ring frequently had transactions with motorcycle clubs and other criminal elements. I will most likely never have an answer to that question. However, that knowledge was the least of my issues from this event.

Once again, I buried yet another traumatizing event. As far as my conscious life was concerned, nothing happened. I lived out the rest of the time in that state staying by our summer home, floating in the water, and avoiding the public as much as possible.

Very shortly after we moved away, I had my first kidney and bladder infection. I was taken to the doctor, who examined me alone.

He was at first stern with me for not coming sooner, asked why I let it get so bad; however, I literally had not felt any of the symptoms until that day. This was due to all the previous deep denial and blocking of incidents.

The doctor then asked me a strange question, one I did not understand, "Where is the baby?" I was shocked and asked him what he meant. He repeated the question frantically, "Where is the baby?!" He then explained to me that my cervix was blue, which only happens during or closely following a pregnancy.

I looked at him in disbelief and declared, "I am a virgin!" Can you imagine the predicament and confusion that doctor was in? There were no precise reporting procedures for this type of thing, no public training; rape awareness was not on the radar.

It was not until decades later that I looked up what a blue cervix was and learned that it is associated with pregnancy. As an adult, I asked my mother about this doctor appointment and she said she could never understand why the doctor came out of the room and adamantly told her to get me on birth control! I later named the little one that I lost Lovely. To this day, I have no idea if I miscarried or what happened. I have a slight memory of my boyfriend accompanying me to the back door of a medical facility. It leaves me wondering about what took place.

I have experienced flashbacks from this event that were incredibly physically painful, and of not knowing where I was. Thinking I was back there, on a picnic table being restrained and brutalized, I was sobbing loudly and trying to crawl away from them. Meanwhile, my husband, David, heard me sobbing and rushed to my side saying my name and telling me where I was. He recognized the all too familiar symptoms of a flashback and leapt to action. He knew he had to call me back into the present.

Flashbacks are horrifically random and can intrude into your life at any time. Sometimes I can identify what sets one off and other times I have no idea why or what detonated it. It is incredibly unnerving to experience flashbacks! I am grateful that every time I have experienced one, David has been with me. I feel empathy for my fellow survivors who have had to endure flashbacks while alone. I am not sure how they are able to bring themselves back into the present, but they inevitably do. Survivors are tough as nails!

Upon returning to the boarding school after that summer, my faith was shattered! I was confused and shamed and hurt. God either did not love me or He did not care about me and He certainly did not protect me. I began down an angry path of rebellion. I was back at the same boarding school but returned as a different person than the one they knew in my junior year. I was in so much emotional pain. I did not know what to do with all the feelings I had inside. I just wanted to numb them. I began to mess around with street drugs. I was not addicted but just looking for escape. This got me kicked out of the school and into another city where my parents had relocated to. Unforeseen by all involved, I was literally being sent directly into the hands of the very ring that had been awaiting the day for easier access to me.

I will attempt to explain the workings of many trafficking rings and specifically the one I dealt with in the Heartland. I personally have met others trafficked by these rings in the smaller populated portions of our nation and it seems they are all run in similar ways.

Having been abused so young, I was the perfect target. Somehow, they instinctively picked me out or possibly the person who first abused me at age four also had connections with the ring. When I was six years old, the ring began the grooming process more intentionally. While still very young, I was never left untouched sexually for any lengthy periods of time due to the fact that the ring operated in so many communities within a multi-state area.

Whenever they could get their hands on me in a community, I was pulled aside and touched, raped, photographed, or filmed by numerous individuals involved with the ring. This was and is so common in Heartland USA, that it is terrifying to know the truth of it. There were certain individuals who maintained an interest in me nearly everywhere we moved, whether in person or via connections. I was being "built" by an assembly line of handlers, each one adding their part to me until their product (me) was ready to be turned out.

By age 17, I was incredibly rebellious and difficult for my parents to manage. I was a senior in high school and I knew that lawfully I could move out by the time I turned 18. I threw that in my parents' face a few too many times and they kicked me out when I had only a few months left before graduation. I already had a part time job plus only two classes that were required in my last semester.

This was the perfect opportunity to be all too available and unmonitored. My introduction to being actively trafficked began within days of moving into my apartment. Another "advantage" for the ring was that I was able to excuse myself from my classes whenever needed. Relatively unchecked, alone, and living with a very relaxed schedule made me highly accessible.

While writing this book, I spoke to one of my very dearest friends from that period in my life and he said that I became very elusive. He said I would hang out with our friends here and there, and then disappear for days or weeks at a time. He was never sure what I was up to or where I was. Sharing with him about the trafficking answered some questions and filled in some blanks for him as to what was going on with me back then. His reaction to this information was both sadness and anger.

Once I turned 18, I would hang out with friends at a bar for a brief period of time while we would be engaging in conversation and then I would simply disappear. Anyone who has lived within the bar scene knows that people rarely keep track of one another unless you have shared a vehicle. Individuals come and go throughout any given evening without notice. It is generally assumed that you are bar hopping. This made it easy for members of the ring to come regularly for me in the bars. They simply needed to walk up to me and speak a code phrase or literally escort me out the back doors.

Most of the time, I knew better than to resist, plus there was something about being approached in public by them that invoked extreme shame. This shame caused me to respond quickly to their demands and code phrases so as to get everything out of the public eye quickly. I was subconsciously concerned that someone I knew would observe what was happening and my shame would be out in the open. I was taught very young that no one would ever believe that it was force and I would be the one blamed. Convincingly they reminded me throughout the years that not only was I expendable, but my reputation would be forever tarnished if exposed. Unfortunately, this deep belief within me made it a very simple process to apprehend me in public without even laying a hand on me until we were outside the doors.

However, shame was not the only thing motivating me to respond in the way that I did. I was unaware of the power of trauma-based mind control based on the use of specific code words or phrases. Mind control is not something new; it is as old as sin. Trauma-based mind control has been around for centuries with some evidence dating it back to ancient times. We need only to look at recent history to find the evidence that it was a technique utilized by our very own government agencies beginning in the 1950's with outcomes which were used to "render an individual subservient to an imposed will or control."[1]

If an individual has others pointing out contrived faults or treating them as unworthy to be in the company of others, they will soon begin to believe that there is something wrong within themselves. It is that old saying that if you tell a person they are stupid long enough, eventually they will become or behave stupid.

I recognize that this is oversimplifying the incredibly complex aspects of trauma-based mind control. Trauma-based mind control

---

[1] "Mind-Control Studies Had Origins in Trial of Mindszenty, 1977-08-02," New York Times, https://www.wanttoknow.info/mind controlnewsarticles, [06/26/2018]

is burned into a person through the use of drugs, extreme repetitive torture, and mind-altering trauma. Hopefully you can begin to understand why it works so well and perhaps conceive of its potential to cause a person to dissociate and bend to the will of the enforcers. True dissociation rarely looks like it is portrayed in the movies where the characters are depicted as dissociated so completely that they have several different personalities, different names, different lives, different homes, etc. In reality, most dissociation is more common than most people realize, and it is much less dramatic.

NATURE OF THE BEAST

Ring trafficking seems to be less publicized than other forms of trafficking and even largely overlooked by educating entities. I am uncertain as to why, but perhaps it is due to the fact that so few escape or survive to talk about it. It may also be linked to the fact that those heading up trafficking rings are nearly always respected, high profile, wealthy, philanthropic, community-engaged, influential people. Additionally, it may be more difficult to pin down due to its ties to organized crime, other organizations, and cults. I would venture to say that much of what happens with ring trafficking looks the same wherever it is operating.

However, ring trafficking is rampant in Heartland USA. Rural America needs to become aware. Turning a blind eye has happened for far too long for fear of what we cannot control, fear of what we do not understand, or fear of reprisal.

While many statistics discuss pimp-controlled trafficking, gang-controlled trafficking, and Romeo pimps, they often fail to acknowledge the enormous number involved in ring trafficking. My personal experience is that roughly one third of the survivors I have spoken with were ring trafficked.

Ring trafficking is very organized and crosses state lines. They are often part of the sex trafficking "pipe-lines" that run across this nation. Due to its very nature, it is difficult to escape. The adage, "you can run, but you can't hide," is very real.

Rings are very networked, undercover, secretive, protected, and lucrative. They use guerilla tactics, torture, violence, imprison-ment, gangs, law enforcement, threats, and snatch-and-grabs to keep their victims hypervigilant, afraid, and obedient.

While the media covers trafficking rings where stings have been set up and victims are being taken across country or from one country to another, few discuss the type of ring that operate right under their noses, in their own neighborhoods. The information about these hometown rings is not readily available.

Yet, these rings are operating nearly everywhere, and are seemingly untouchable! Most victims/survivors are unwilling to mention names or organizations due to fear and shame. The shame comes from the fact that victims are perpetrated on while they are very young. Then they are groomed for lengthy periods and turned out to be trafficked. It confuses the issue of where the guilt belongs in the minds of the victims and the general public. Most people have difficulty grasping the immense control a ring can have over an individual. It is my hope that telling my story will aid in educating about this type of trafficking.

Ring trafficking, by its very nature, is covert and difficult to pin down. For instance, I have no arrest record. Of course not! This is another way that ring trafficking is different from many other forms of sex trafficking. Rings like to keep their slaves clean in every way! Clean of tattoos, clean of too many scars (that cannot be covered), clean of disease, clean of arrest records, clean work resumes, etc. Everything must look like the slave is okay and living a normal life. The people involved in the rings must never have their names, customers, reputations, or operations exposed. Secrecy is everything! This is why they operate so smoothly and undetected.

Survivors in heavily populated areas often have to walk the streets (a.k.a. the track or the blade) in the bigger cities. However, in Heartland USA, that would be nearly impossible as it would be immediately noticed due to lower populations. I was forced to stand on a street corner, but only once, in the middle of the night as a test. Yet it was all a setup, including the trick who picked me up. It was just another punishment for my insubordination.

Being punished is very ritualistic and routine for most sex trafficking victims regardless of who the handlers are. There was constant trauma of not knowing what would anger or disappoint the pimp/handler/trafficker. There were certain rules that you learned quickly, but others were constantly changing. It is never a one-time event; it is constant in your life both day and night while in slavery.

Due to these horrendous rules, I had amnesia barriers set up all over the place! Facing one small thing could unravel an entire system of blocked memories of the most horrific years! I could not, would not, should not remember or speak of it as it was programmed into me: "Do not remember!" This is brainwashing. Many traffickers will use every possible means to make you forget. The set-up is especially sinister with trafficking rings, familial pimping, cults, or organized crime rings as they begin with intentionally grooming children as young as they can get to them.

Romeo pimps are another category in which they lure a female by pretending to love and care for them, then eventually force them into sexual slavery. These diverse types often work together as the money to be made by the traffickers is outrageous! It is easy money to them, while it is hell to the victim.

Obedience to your handlers means making the clientele happy whatever the cost to you personally. Disobedience or even a defiant look can get you punished. The punishments can last for hours or days. Your family members are threatened. Your children can be held hostage. They often intentionally force drugs on you with the intention of getting you addicted. Your life is threatened regularly.

The torture is so severe that most survivors fracture/fragment into altered states in order to survive the ordeals. This is medically known as Dissociative Identity Disorder (DID). If you did not learn this survival skill, you may never make it through with your mind intact. This skill is vital. It also takes an intelligent and creative mind to implement this system of survival.

For commercial sex trafficking, I have read that the victims are often intentionally chosen who have high IQs and creative minds. It takes great brilliance to fragment enough to survive the things one goes through in trafficking. Without this gift, the victim would most likely need to be institutionalized for life. Yet, while in the life, the handler/pimps/traffickers tell you the very opposite of the truth about your intelligence in order to brainwash you even further. You are told repeatedly that you are stupid, that you cannot do anything else, that this is all you are made for, that nobody is going to ever want you, etc.

I was sex trafficked in all its forms: porn magazines; porn movies; prostituted out of hotels and at private parties; escort services; and private strip clubs from ages 17 to 21 years old.

They used many different drugs on me such as: chloroform to knock me out followed by ammonia to reawaken me; Black Beauties which cause both sexual arousal and amnesia (these were their drugs of choice that were force-fed to me like candy); cocaine; angel dust; Quaaludes; amphetamines; and LSD. I was also provided speed so that I could be awake enough to work a regular job during the day. The shear exhaustion and assault on my body from these drugs alone cannot be measured. My body was not my own, it was taken, and the blood of that near decimation is on the hands of many.

I do not have the actual names of most of these individuals as they rarely used their real names. This elite group worked out of a several-state area that was their circuit. They would bring in the "trainers" from major metropolitan cities to be certain that obedience was in place. This was mind-bending torture, pain and pleasure confusion control, life-threatening situations, gang rapes, and humiliation. It put you in your place. Survival became paramount.

Understand this—no one wants to be raped over and over every day. Most, if not all, trafficking survivors never receive one dime for their suffering. It is not a job; do not call it the "oldest profession!" It is slavery. Do not call us prostitutes! We were prostituted. I have mentioned this before, but I want readers and survivors to really grasp this. We were prostituted! There is generally no choice involved on the part of the survivor.

To those who have paid for sex, I hope you hear me. Those who are trapped in that life do not want you; they are not hot for you; they are not happy to be making money this way; and they do not get to keep the money you give them. They are in physical and emotional pain and torment. They are role playing to save their own lives or the lives of someone they love. They are faking their way through their time with you so that they will survive another day! I speak from experience. The same can be said for all forms of Commercial Sexual Exploitation (CSE).

God, I pray that You expose those who are intentionally involved in harming fellow human beings via sex trafficking. Please bring a radical change to our understanding and handling of this enormous burden in our midst. Guide us to wise plans and insider information. Light the path for us!

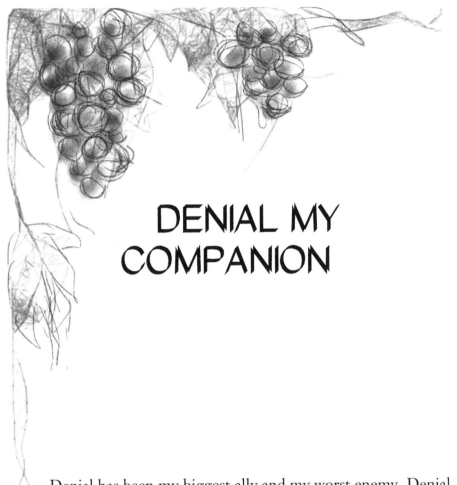

DENIAL MY COMPANION

Denial has been my biggest ally and my worst enemy. Denial kept me from hurting and yet kept me captive. It had leaked into virtually every area of my life. The thing about denial is that you don't/can't/won't recognize that you have it! You are in denial about its very existence.

My denial has often been mistaken for toughness, aloofness, or even at its worst, callousness. I call it jaded. Jaded is to be made dull, apathetic, or even cynical by experience or by seeing too much of something.

Denial began early in my life—which I generally only ascribe to myself and my issues. Whereas with others, I have always been extra sensitive to and eager to help them in their crisis. I am almost hypervigilant to noticing someone else's downcast countenance and will seek to get them the help they may need. It is the same with other people's health issues. I notice them, often before they do.

When it comes to myself, however, my senses are dulled. I never noticed certain ailments in my life until they were at nearly life and death status. It was not uncommon to have doctors say to me, "Why didn't you come in here sooner?"

My response was always, "Well, I didn't really notice it," or "It didn't hurt that bad, I barely felt it," or "I figured it would just go away." I can see where I learned this way of dealing—well, this way of NOT dealing. Now that I am no longer in denial about my past, I can see things more clearly.

I must say that, in many ways it was much easier to live in denial land. Having to notice when someone or something hurts my feelings is not fun. I daily fight not moving back into the land where I am comfortable. It feels better not to feel.

That is not how God designed us, however. He knows that when we do not feel, it becomes just like the illnesses that I did not feel, a festering disease that will take you out if not dealt with.

I teach and counsel others that just tucking something away and putting a Band-Aid over it allows the infection to burrow in and turn to gangrene. One must tear off the Band-Aid and cleanse the wound for proper healing to occur. Oddly, I thought denial was a way of dealing with my past appropriately, and in a sense, it was. Denial was so huge in my life that I honestly had no conscious memory of the things that were causing gangrene.

Denial was partially my choice, but mostly it was intentionally forced upon me by those who had been evil to me. There is a type of trauma-based mind control that happens when you have the type of life I lived. Through this, those in charge of your memories, so to speak, specifically and succinctly inflict enough trauma to cause amnesia barriers. When you are broken enough and traumatized enough, your mind succumbs. It can be considered brain washing.

Trauma-based mind control is atrocious in all its variables. It cannot be prepared for and it cannot be fought, not even on a conscious level. This is where the traffickers break you intentionally and it is even more deeply imbedded than traumatic dissociation. The only way to freedom from its clutches is to be removed from it and be retrained. You need to acquire new behavior patterns and habits by eliminating their programming and replacing it with truth, plus surrounding yourself with caring people, and really just starting over.

These tormenters were like snipers with skills so precise that they knew exactly where to apply threats, torture, and shame. They also knew how to place land mines that when they "exploded", I was in a state of shock and dismay, never knowing where the next land mine was going to be.

What made them happy one day would cause them anger and displeasure the next. I did not understand this then. It was a double bind, no-win situation, intentionally set to cause mental distress that would lead to my being unable to trust my own decisions. Once you do not trust yourself, you are more easily mind controlled.

This set-up is true of any type of ongoing abuse. If you have never been there, it is hard to understand the absolute control that they have over your thinking. It is the same syndrome that happens to prisoners of war who are kept long term. They break you until you can no longer think your own thoughts, until the person you were is buried deep inside. I once told my husband in a healing session that I felt broken like shards of glass, each shard having very sharp edges.

Bringing the pieces together is a key component in progressing forward in life for a survivor. I do not necessarily mean these parts must all integrate, so much as teaching the remaining fragments of the mind to work together as one. A fragmented mind sounds frightening. As a society, we have done a great disservice by not addressing this issue more frequently. In fact, we ALL dissociate to some degree. The levels to which we do this are dependent upon our life's trauma.

Let me attempt to normalize this for you. Have you ever found yourself driving across the city and upon arriving at your destination you realize that you do not recall any of the stoplights along the way? During that drive, you were unaware of the mundane road which you traveled, and your mind went elsewhere. Perhaps you were thinking about groceries, or a disagreement you had with someone that morning, but you arrived safely without an accident or a ticket. You dissociated slightly out of shear boredom. We can do this while doing dishes, mowing the lawn, or cooking, and yet you are able to function highly in this state and accomplish what needs to be accomplished.

Let's increase the dissociation a little now. Imagine that you hate going to the dentist (apologies to those who are dentists), but it is a necessary appointment and so you go. You are feeling uptight, uneasy, and maybe hoping for a little medicinal relief ahead of time. At this point, you are thinking you would rather be anywhere else. You get into the dentist's chair and you begin a routine familiar to yourself each time you sit in that chair. You begin to intentionally focus on something else, anything else. You tune out the sound of the drill, the smell of the instruments, and the mask on the dentist's face. Very soon you are thinking about a trip to the beach you would like to take, maybe the outfit you are going to wear tonight, or perhaps that deer you are hoping to bag this year. Before you know it, the dentist is done, and you survived once again. When you get up, you realize you have just passed two hours of time! You wipe a little sweat off your brow, a sigh of relief, settle the bill, and leave.

We all dissociate on some level. I am not going to go into all the differing psychological definitions or descriptions for dissociating. I will, however, give you my belief regarding severe trauma, which nearly always inevitably causes extreme dissociation.

Dissociation in trauma is a gift from God to His children. When a child suffers untold trauma, especially where there is a threat to the life of that child, they will most certainly dissociate. This is the only way to go through the type of trauma that many of us have suffered at the hands of others and to still be sane.

If I had to stay present in my most traumatizing situations, I would not have survived with my mind intact. I am grateful that the Lord gives the brains of children the ability to dissociate.

I am also grateful to be living in a time when psychology and therapists are recognizing the reality of dissociation. Some of the most respected people in society have had great trauma and were able to become who they are due to their ability to dissociate from those things which were too horrifying to stay fully present for.

In studying the dissociation of our living Prisoners of War, it has been discovered that many have lost memory of some or all of what occurred during their torture. Despite physical evidence, these war heroes are not able to recall what happened and have also lost portions of time.

This is a healthy response to trauma—it is a lifesaving response. It should carry no shame. Not dissociating in extreme trauma can contribute greatly to the absolute breaking of the mind in which the person is lost forever.

One of the battles in society has been that we do not want to publicly address dissociation nor is it accepted as normal. Dissociation is practically whispered rather than brought into the light and addressed freely. If we could grasp this more readily and understand its beauty in survival, we could more fully accept ourselves.

I say it plainly and without shame, I suffered horrendous trauma and I was blessed to have dissociation with amnesia. Yes, I did mean to use the term "blessed." The Lord gifted my brain with the ability to dissociate. I am truly blessed to have had that ability and I am grateful to God for it. Many of my memories were partially blocked and some were fully blocked for many years. This too is more common than people admit to.

If you are a safe person for someone to tell, they may eventually initiate a conversation with you to share their hazy and partially blocked memories. They may tell you of the big long blank times in their lives where there seems to be no memories or only fragments of memories. How many people do you personally know who have mentioned that they really do not remember their childhood? There is generally a reason for this.

> "Research suggests that, along with emotionality, the coherence of a memory contributes to its longevity in memory. The extent to which an experience is understood in a meaningful way affects the likelihood that it will be incorporated into the permanent repertoire of the events of our life."[2]

This research explains why trauma victims have extensive parts and pieces of memories. We simply cannot make sense of the harm done to us by others. It cannot be understood because it is not acceptable or normal behavior on the part of the perpetrators.

Those blocked memories will stay hidden until a person feels safe with their environment, more specifically, with the people they are closest to. Getting a do-over is a wonderful gift that this life has to offer us, no matter what age we are or how long we have been trapped. Personally, as I began to feel trust and greater love for my husband, David, my amnesia barriers began to come down. Little by little, my brain began to leak the dark secrets of my past. All the places where I had those partial memories and wondered what happened next began to fill in. A pattern began to form, and voila! My life began to make sense.

The first restored memory was not my first trauma. I have yet to understand why my first memory came to me out of chronological

---

[2] Krystine I Batcho PhD, "What Your Oldest Memories Reveal About You" Psychology Today https://www.psychologytoday.com/us/blog/longing-nostalgia/201504/what-your-oldest-memories-reveal-about-you [06/13/2018]

order of events. Some of it may have been environmental. I was safe with my husband, and I had watched a scene on a television show that emulated something that had happened to me during one of the gang rapes when I was 13 years old. While I had no conscious memory of the original event, my subconscious held it all.

This is where it all began, my journey backward into my past, so that I could move forward in my life. Remember the gangrene I mentioned earlier? I had a lot of it, rotting on the inside, that I was not consciously aware of. God knew my husband was the right person to walk through it with me. Little did we know how long the journey would be or how horrific. Thankfully, God also knew to give me only one memory at a time. If it had all opened up at once, I am uncertain that we could have endured it.

These episodes of remembering can take a lot of time to get through and they take a persistent commitment to receiving healing. What good would it be to remember and then just bury it again?

I want to take a moment here and pray for you. Lord, if there are any who are reading this who have serious trauma and suspect dissociation, I ask that they release it into Your capable hands. God give them the ability to let it go until You know they are ready to remember. If there are any who are reading this that are dissociated and do not have even a slight clue, I entrust them into Your great love to bring out what needs brought out in Your perfect timing.

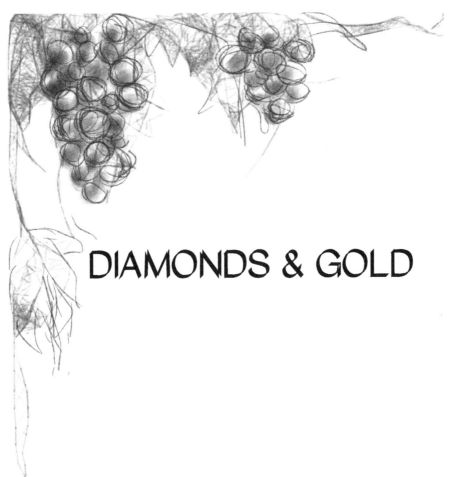

DIAMONDS & GOLD

In a dream I heard and saw the Lord say, "When you cease to mine for gold, then the gold will attenuate, and you will see the diamonds." I was in a cave looking around. There was gold that was everywhere, as I began to look at the dirt walls and ceiling my focus turned to the diamonds in the dirt. The gold did not disappear, but the diamonds were more appealing, and I could grab handfuls of diamonds from the ceiling within the dirt. I could also find them in the dirt below. What was God saying to me?

Attenuate was not a word I was very familiar with and certainly not a word I commonly used. It means to weaken or reduce in force, intensity, effect, quantity, or value.

Gold

I began to think about gold vs. diamonds. Gold is soft, diamonds are hard. Melting gold by fire is done to remove the impurities. We generally think of gold in the Bible as related to when a person is purified by fire and the impurities are removed which results in holiness. Those impurities are useless and contaminated waste product that must be removed from metal in the refining process. It has no value and its presence diminishes the value of any metal it is in. For metal to have value, the dross (impurities) must be removed. In many passages, the Bible uses the analogy of dross to show how we are polluted by its presence.

Gold is one of the most precious metals. "I counsel you to buy from Me gold refined in the fire…" (Revelation 3:18).

When we first come to a relationship with God, most of us have very visible impurities, like drinking, cursing, drugging, stealing, etc. The longer we walk with the Lord, the less impurities we have as we are being transformed daily from glory to glory!

Diamonds

Diamonds are much more valuable per ounce than gold. They are the hardest minerals in the world and one of the most chemically stable substances ever known to mankind. They really are nearly invincible as one of the most precious gemstones. The beauty of a diamond emerges in the faceting process that allows the brilliance of its internal light to be exposed. Diamonds are created under extreme pressure up to 120 miles below the surface of the earth. Can you imagine the pressure, the darkness, the isolation in those circumstances? Imagine the distance from anyone who could truly appreciate or come to understand this difficult process let alone discover that they are hidden there.

Those who suffer in the faith are described in the book of Peter in much the same way that diamonds are created. This verse describes the same process.

> In all this you greatly rejoice, though now for a little while you may have had to suffer grief in all kinds of trials. These have come so that the proven genuineness of your faith—of greater worth than gold, which perishes even though refined by fire—may result in praise, glory, and honor when Jesus Christ is revealed. 1 Peter 1:6-7

I did not know these facts before having my dream. How interesting that the Lord showed me the diamonds among the dirt. So descriptive of my life and of the lives of most survivors. We are gems of high quality to the Lord, but nearly lost in the dirt. The higher the pressure and the higher the temperature, the greater the quality of diamond, giving it superior structural qualities, optical purity, and transparency. Diamonds in scripture represent stability, brilliancy, virtue, and right standing with God.

Diamond in the Rough

This term is commonly used to refer to someone that has hidden characteristics that are exceptional and may have future potential, but currently lack the finishing touches that would make them stand out from the rest. This phrase is a metaphor which relates to the fact that naturally occurring diamonds are ordinary and dull at first glance. Their true beauty is only recognized through the cutting and polishing process.[3]

Perfecting

A master diamond cutter once told me that the master craftsman cuts away the impurities and imperfections and begins the process of faceting, so that at every possible angle light is reflected. Once a diamond is cut, light strikes its surface which is in turn absorbed by the diamond. I do not understand much about physics, but I enjoy that it teaches us that the same amount of light that is absorbed is also reflected.

As people are the diamonds in this dream, then we can understand that the Lord is the Master diamond cutter and He is carefully faceting us. The Lord will be able to look into every facet that He cuts and see His face reflected. The chisel used by the diamond cutter is of the hardest and sharpest material. It is the only material that can cut through a diamond. What tool is God using in your life? Is it a person, a situation, an illness, or a loss? The tool will be sharp; it will be precise. The Master Craftsman, with a painful, but loving chisel, is busy at work.

---

[3] Ainz, Urban Dictionary, January, 24, 2006, https://www.urbandictionary.com/define.php?term=Diamond%20in%20they%20rough [7/6/2018]

In the case of trafficking, the chisel is NOT the perpetrators of these crimes. God does not pick up sinful tools as His intentional instruments. However, God will take the evil done to individuals and turn it to good. Those who suffer the greatest pressure, the most agonizing trials, the severest losses, the most mind-numbing isolation, trauma, torture, and the most debilitating infirmities are being carefully formed in that unbearably lonely terrain. You, my survivor friends, are gems in the hand of the Lord. You are His treasures. Diamonds in the dirt are overlooked by the eyes of mankind, but the eyes of the Lord are upon you.

Many people believe that God will never give you more than you can handle. God will, in fact, frequently allow more than we can handle on our own, which in turn causes us to come to Him with our issues and our needs. Joseph, the Apostle Paul, King David, Job, and Daniel were not spared this process. Beatings, loneliness, incarcerations, loss, suffering, prolonged illnesses, isolation, and loss of reputation all became a part of the faceting process which shaped them into models for us. We are in good company.

We can trust not only God's timeless skill, but His craftmanship, whose sense of touch and hand-eye coordination perfect the diamond's final form. A perfected diamond will have the ability to inhale more light and exhale fire, sparkle, and brightness like no other. Anyone who knows me knows I love sparkle!

Applying the final polish produces a diamond as nearly perfect as any jewel on earth and certainly more universally desired than any other gemstone. I have rarely found more perfectly faceted, fiery, sparkly individuals than trafficking survivors who have been rescued from the life and have begun their healing journey. Survivors understand the hardening process more intimately than most persons on this planet.

Both gold and diamonds are desired. Both are precious. In the dream, the gold was not gone, it was still there; however, I was being summoned to notice the diamonds now, to take my focus off the gold. Why? Gold is about holiness and purification. I sense the Lord is saying that many of us who are in process are looking to find what still needs cleansed from us and perhaps even trying to purify ourselves more, when what God is doing in us has less to do with ridding us of sin or impurities, but rather He is battle hardening us. He is giving us strength, courage, fortitude, and determination. Begin looking for the diamonds!

He is causing us to be multi-faceted, that whatever side of us is viewed, a beautiful sparkle will be visible, that our every facet will reflect the Son, that at every possible angle, we will be beautiful, hard, precious, precise, sharp, and strong. We will be an army, ready, chiseled, and fashioned by the Master's hand. He is the general of this army; We do not go into battle alone!

"Have I not commanded you? Be strong and courageous. Do not be afraid; do not be discouraged, for the Lord your God will be with you wherever you go" (Joshua 1:9).

The tools of God are plentiful and frequently disguised. Often, they are painful, just as the comparison of the diamond cutter chiseling facets into a diamond until He sees His reflection in each facet. This is what our Father does with us. A chisel is a very sharp, pointy, and strong tool. It does not bend; it accomplishes what it was set to do.

Please do not misunderstand me to say that God is the one who caused my abuse in order to make me a better person (a diamond). God has nothing to do with wickedness, except to turn it around for our good after the fact. I want to clarify that the evil within the hearts of men and women which caused me so much pain did not come from the Creator. God is the one who brought about my healing and in THAT process, He refined me. God chiseled me by helping me remember painful memories, guiding me to forgive my torturers, and giving me the strength to help others. Without God's refinement, I would still be a mess.

I have a lovely friend, my survivor sister, Ann Marie Babbs.[4] She refers to dissociated parts as "facets." I love that! I have begun lovingly using this term as well. Using the term "facets" in the context of dissociation is describing the parts of us that suffered much, where the reflection of Jesus is seen in unique and differing ways. God loves these facets and He values their existence. What a Creator we have!

Can we be fully integrated when we have been so thoroughly faceted/dissociated? This is a question I am frequently asked by trauma survivors. My answer is that integration is not the priority or goal in my mind. The priority and the goal is healing the wounds to the extent that a survivor can live a normal and functional life. There are many survivors who are dissociated due to past trafficking trauma that lead huge organizations. They are top level trainers who use their expertise to educate law enforcement, officials, medical personnel, etc. They work within the judicial system; they hold public office, they are therapists, they are doctors, they are people.

---

[4] Ann Marie Babbs, VP of Business Operations at the WCWT Center (We Care so We're There Center) and Executive Director of the Springhaven Home in Ohio. She was also awarded the 2017 Steele Magnolia Award.

QUICKSAND

Most survivors deal with some phobias. Mine has been severe claustrophobia. Thankfully, I am mostly free of that. I used to get into elevators and would check out every detail, look for the emergency buttons, never get into one alone, and see where the screws on the ceiling were in case I needed to climb out. I still do not enjoy riding in them, but I no longer scan the entire elevator for an emergency exit strategy, and I will even ride on them alone if necessary.

Any enclosed areas that do not have a window that I can climb out of are still uncomfortable for me. I also always used to have difficulty breathing while in tight spaces. Major improvements have occurred for me with these issues, but I look forward to the day of being completely free from them.

Since the first time I saw someone stuck in quicksand in a movie, it has terrified me. I have never actually seen quicksand, but the idea of it sounds worse than nearly anything else I can imagine happening in the wild.

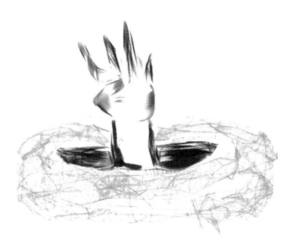

My husband, David, however, has physically experienced being caught in quicksand! When he was a young boy, he and his father and friends were walking along the river. David had gotten quite a distance away from them on his own when he stepped into it. He immediately began to sink and was completely stuck. He knew that he was not to fight, and he knew that the more he moved, the quicker it would suck him down. Yelling for his father and friends, to his dismay, it took a while for them to hear him. By the time they heard David yelling and came running, he was already in it up to his neck! Thankfully, they were able to pull him out in time. His memory of this incident is still very vivid.

David is not emotionally scarred from that incident, nor does he have claustrophobia or any other phobia. He recounts that his only fear in the moment was that there could be a cow corpse underneath him and he did not want his feet to touch it. Ha! Gross!

Quicksand

That certainly would not have been on the list of my fears in that moment, rather, smothering comes to mind.

Quicksand usually consists of sand or clay and salt that has become waterlogged. The ground looks solid, but when you step on it, the sand begins to liquefy. This reminds me of being sucked into the slavery life of being trafficked. If the dangers were apparent, virtually no one would ever step onto THAT ground!

As I did some research on how to escape quicksand, I found some of it to be so relatable. For instance,

> After throwing off any extra gear: resist the urge to wiggle your legs. Quicksand liquefies whenever there's movement. As you sink, your weight pushes water from the sand. With the water gone, the sand thickens, creating a vacuum that tugs you down. You are sinking. You are sinking because the sand around your legs has lost water. But if that water can return, the sand's grip should loosen. That is your route to escape and the only way to do that is to move. [5]

Right here, I was thinking, "Wait, move?" It just stated that you are to resist wiggling. As I continued to read, however, it explained that it is about HOW one moves that makes the difference in being able to escape.

This next step of escape is quite bizarre in its similarity to being trafficked.

> Time to redistribute your weight. If you're ankle or knee deep, slowly sit down. If you're waist deep, lean on your

---

[5] "How to Escape Quicksand." http://mentalfloss.com/article/51826 /how-escape-quicksand [May 10, 2018]

back. Don't panic about sinking—a pit of quicksand is like a swimming pool. You'll sink if you stand, but you'll float if you spread out on your back. [6]

I hate to be so graphic, but the reality of sex trafficking is that you must keep doing what you are doing *on your back* until the opportunity is presented to get out! You simply will not survive otherwise. I have seen others nearly beaten to death when resisting. I have received those beatings as well. I am not certain who survived and who did not of those that were owned by this ring.

Being trafficked relates to being stuck in quicksand for me on so many levels. When owned by a trafficking ring, you are desperately sinking in over your head. Just like quicksand, you cannot fight noticeably, or it gets worse for you. You must think your way out. One minute can feel like a thousand years during this part. You begin imagining your escape from day one. I did not actually get away from the active trafficking for four years. Yet, I never lost the hope that maybe one day I would get out. However, pondering this on a daily basis made everything feel hopeless.

I would compare this to a "no-win situation" or "choose the lesser of two evils." A term that some of us use when referring to this is a "double bind." The definition of a double bind is a situation in which a person is confronted with two irreconcilable demands or a choice between two undesirable courses of action. Basically, no matter what you choose, you lose. You are forced to choose daily from awful "options." If you do not do this awful thing, then this more awful thing will happen to you. This is part of why so many

---

[6] "How to Escape Quicksand." http://mentalfloss.com/article/51826 /how-escape-quicksand [May 10, 2018]

survivors do not self-identify as being trafficked. They made a "choice" between one awful thing and another, sometimes many times a day. Obviously, it is really no choice, but the mind is being bent and broken hours on end nearly daily.

This explains why once a survivor has escaped, we find it hard to say "no" to people and to doing things. Most survivors are battle-hardened over-achievers. We can be the best employees because we were conditioned to work long hours. We know what it is to dig in and get things done. This awful thing done to us can be turned into an attribute, if we remember to give ourselves rest. It can be our downfall, if we do not choose rest and learn that saying "no" is okay and sometimes vital.

My sisters and brothers who have been forced to work the streets have an added issue to contend with, which is that of competition due to the quotas they must meet. When stepping into square life, competing with others must be unlearned. Burned into the minds of those who are victims of trauma-based control is that competing to win is survival. Please have patience and compassion in this for those that have come out of working the streets.

It is all exhausting. Our bodies were not intended for this abuse, nor were our minds. If it were not for the amazing work of God in my life, I am not sure I would be here. If not for the hope that was built deep in my soul, I may have given up long ago.

My husband and I have often noted that I see the glass half full and he sees the glass half empty. I am relatively certain that this view of the glass being half full played a huge role in my eventual escape. I do not know where that hope came from. It must have been instilled into my character by God so that I would fight to live and not give up and die in that life. This is not to say that those with the same hope do not die there. Many die fighting to escape right up to the very end. My heart aches daily for those whose lives are lost in the trafficking life.

Please join me in praying that hope is kept alive in all those who are still trapped in the quicksand that is trafficking in all its forms: forced labor, prostitution, escort services, pornographic films, pornographic magazines, and exotic dancing/stripping.

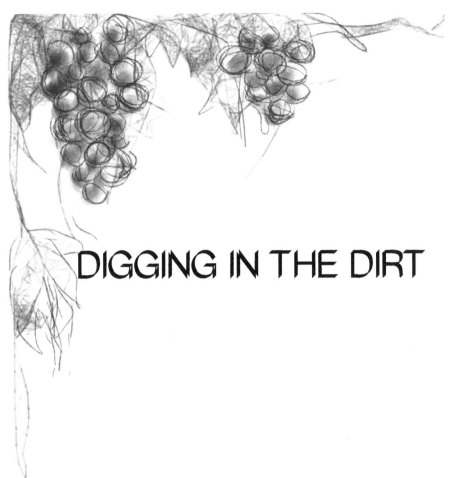

DIGGING IN THE DIRT

After pondering the idea of being a diamond in the dirt, I look back and really cannot believe THAT was once my life—but it was— all of it. The ugliness is inescapable, especially as far as memories go. God really had to pull me out of the dirt and begin reshaping me into the person He wanted me to be. I am so grateful that He has been willing to work so patiently and tenderly with every facet He wanted carved into who I am. I am a work in progress. Yet, aren't we all? Some of us were just buried deeper in the dirt.

There are areas in my life that could be likened to a diamond. Virtually all diamonds contain "beauty marks" that are small imperfections inside the diamond. The diamond is, nevertheless, still incredibly valuable with these marks. In fact, a diamond's unique imperfections can be a great identifier. Similar to snowflakes or fingerprints, no two diamonds are exactly alike. In a higher quality diamond, these marks are not visible to the naked eye. They often remind me of scars that are identifiers, too. One cannot endure being subjected to sex trafficking and come out unscarred, generally in both body and soul. It is an identifier.

My understanding of God is that His very own Son, Jesus, was scarred from the things He endured on the cross. He was given a glorified body, yet He still carries the scars on His hands and feet. This has made Him so very precious and so very valuable.

Some marks may always be with me, but they helped form me. While they get less and less noticeable each year, they are nevertheless something I am aware of, even though they are not noticeable to another's eye.

In the same manner, lingering residue of my trauma may always be with me. I am never certain when I may run into someone who knew me back then. This is disconcerting, but very real. As a survivor, I deal with flashbacks, never knowing when I may experience one, though they have become rarer as time has passed. Yet, when they do happen, they generally set me into a state of hypervigilance which can last for days. Nightmares are always hiding in the shadows waiting to give me an unwanted "surprise" from time to time. I hate waking with my heart racing, my body reacting, and having to remind myself where I am and that I am okay. I generally reach over and touch my husband for reassurance and to ground myself.

There are for me and most survivors ongoing health issues. Most of us battle autoimmune diseases among other health problems common to survivors. For example, we have significant joint issues like football players do. The obvious difference is that we do not get the compensation or ongoing benefits of being in the "game." In fact, many survivors have such extensive arrest records that they have difficulty attaining gainful employment, nor can they afford the much-needed mental and physical assistance. The long-term effects are always lurking.

This is not the kind of life one simply puts behind them and moves on from. It is my hope to educate those who give that response or suggestion by bringing understanding of how life-altering trafficking is. The following has not happened to me yet; however, I have heard of this happening to many other survivors when asked to share their story: They are told to make it palatable or upbeat. Palatable?! Upbeat?! It simply is not either of these! You cannot make it pretty or sugar coat it. I have left out a lot in the telling of my story. If I were to write down everything, I would fill a closet full of books. Please, do not tell us to make it palatable. Instead, understand that it is detestable; that is what must be expressed. This is a blight on society that must be stopped! If it is sugar coated, who will hate it enough to fight it?

That type of suppression is one of the unhealthiest approaches in transitioning from survivor to thriver. If we do not fully face what we have been through, we do not fully heal or move forward in life. If we are not accepted fully for where we have come from, then we are partially rejected for something we did not choose. I refuse to settle for partial acceptance. It is all of me or none of me! Yes, all the dirt.

Some will know me deeper than others. Some will know more "dirt." Those are the ones who can truly appreciate the cleansing of the Lord in my life. They know how far I have come. My husband is the one who knows me the most. He is one of a kind. He loves me. He respects me, and yet he knows more dirt than anyone. He expresses a love and admiration that can only be God-given. When he looks at me, he does not see the dirt I came from; he sees the diamond I have become. I am blessed. As my good friend, Gina, reminded me when proofreading this section, "…and this is also how God sees you, Kelly."

People assume that while being trafficked, one lives a glamorous life with furs and diamonds. On the outside, I dressed glamorous for specific situations, especially escort services. In most trafficking situations, the luxuries were all for show to the clientele. When they gifted items to me, they were not mine to keep. I owned nothing.

I was starved nearly every day. I generally weighed between 93 and 95 pounds. If I ever climbed over 95 pounds, I was scolded and reminded to get back on my diet. My diet consisted of a Snickers bar once a day, Coke, and a can of soup. I lived that way for all the years I was trafficked. Family members were so worried I was anorexic. I did not have an eating disorder of my choosing because I could eat anyone under the table, if given the chance! I was allowed to be with family and friends on most holidays as appearances had to be kept up. The wonderful meals during those times were such a luxury!

Most of my clothing was purchased for me by others to wear during my regular work day. All clothing items were purchased for me to wear during my "night and weekend job." Two totally different wardrobes. Two totally different lives. Two totally different people sharing one body. God was aware of both. I was not—at least not consciously. God loved both Kelly of the day and Kelly of the night. God knew how to get to both of me. He would minister to me in my sleep and in my waking hours in order to fully get through my walls. He was willing to go the distance!

As a very high functioning person, I had relatively good day jobs at a young age. Unfortunately, many of my employers were also a part of the trafficking ring. They always had their eye on where I was and what I was doing. Due to family and friends in my life, the façade had to be kept up. It worked well. Few knew. Most of the ones who did know were involved on some level themselves.

While in this trafficking ring, keeping up appearances was just as important as performing perfectly. This is where I hope to dispel any false beliefs about exotic dancers, pornography film "stars," prostitution, and escort services. When and if you have ever watched any of these, you are experiencing the best actors and actresses in any industry. The smiles on the faces look so real that one can almost believe they are enjoying themselves. Let me tell you the dirt behind the scenes without needing to be too explicit.

If there was ever a performance that was not done convincingly, as though you wanted to be there, the consequences were just barely survivable. Free will does not exist in the sex industry, not for those who are trafficked. The trafficking ring that was operating in my area used guerilla tactics to school their victims. One of their favorite schooling tactics was gang rape, which is something no one ever gets accustomed to. It does not get easier or more tolerable when repeated. However, your numbing skills can increase to where they kick in sooner during and after the event.

When watching a film, you can only see what is in front of the camera. You do not see the weapons, the handlers, and the drugs being forced into the performers who are trafficked.

While I was trafficked, some of my "co-stars" were not. Even they were aware of the difference. They knew not to try to interact with me between takes. Others were being paid, while they suspected that I was not. They noticed the handlers, and the drugs being fed to me like candy. Understandably, they feared these people enough to steer clear of obstructing anything going on behind the scenes. To my knowledge, no one dared to try to expose these criminals.

There was one person from my filming days who had the idea to rescue me, but when found out, he was not allowed to film with me again. In fact, that person was led to believe that I had died and that it may have been his fault. It was not until he found me years later that he learned otherwise.

You sometimes see survivors draw a red X on their hand or their social media pages. It has symbolic meaning for many to stamp out trafficking. It is a great message. However, I have not found it personally comfortable to use the red X as my message against trafficking.

For me, the X was another part of schooling and it was meant to symbolize keeping your mouth shut, don't tell. Do not ever tell. I was chained up in a basement for several days with tape over my mouth with a large X drawn across the tape. This was to teach me to be quiet. This was just one of many "taming" events, and a minor one at that. I despise duct tape to this day! They would remove the tape to give me sips from a cup of water occasionally. Enough to keep me alive, but not enough to satisfy the dryness of my mouth and throat. Once the tape was removed, my mouth and throat were raw.

There was no time, however, to pay attention to that as the next part of schooling began immediately—the torture room—filled with instruments, tools, and devices that resembled medieval times along with modern electrical equipment. Cameras were in place to catch it all on film as well. There is no end to their brutality. It is hard to imagine what humans are willing to do to other humans, and sadly much of society would prefer to believe that this is not happening in their own back yards.

I know people prefer not to hear these things, but I want you to know at least enough to HATE trafficking and all that goes with it! I want you to hate the sexual exploitation of human beings at any age. I want you to recognize and acknowledge that most people involved in the sex industry do not choose to be there. I want you to despise modern slavery and to abhor all those who profit from it. I want you to be shocked, even repulsed. It is a fine line, to keep what is written somewhat sterile, and yet to expose the atrocities to a degree that the reader will grasp how horrid, how immensely awful, how disgusting, and how utterly devastating it is.

I have had to experience things that others cannot possibly understand, unless they have lived through being sex trafficked. I have seen the barbaric beatings of other women besides myself when they disobeyed, when they tried to escape, or when they were being schooled. We were not prostitutes. We were being prostituted. We were slaves. Becoming an adult in the life does not free you to choose.

I was not able to escape until I was 21 years old, and many are trapped much longer than I was. Your age is not what distinguishes you as a slave, your captivity does.

Years after having been in that life, I have been to various doctors, for a variety of health issues. On several occasions while receiving x-rays for various issues I have been asked where and when I had previously broken a bone in one place or another within my body. For instance, in a sinus x-ray the doctor told me I had broken my nose badly at some point, he indicated that I must have really had some black eyes with that one. At an ER visit a doctor told me he could see a healed rib from a bad break. Then he questioned me quite a bit because he told me that it was impossible to break that specific rib bone from anything other than a blow from the outside. He asked if I had ever been in a car wreck and broke it—I hadn't. His concern was obvious.

Whenever I am asked when or how these various broken bones happened, sadly, I have no answers for them. I am not sure. The fact is, I do not recall when most of these bones were broken or which incident caused which injury since pain is an everyday thing in that life. If you were to question a former prisoner of war, you might get the same blank response. We do not recall. It was too frequent, too traumatic, too much.

The encouragement is this: I am no longer a slave. Those who forced this upon me and those who continue to force it upon others are the true slaves. They are slaves to their greed and their perversion. They are not free—BUT I AM!

Today I live a radically different life. Unfortunately, that is not true of all survivors. I have a magnificent husband, a beautifully large family, great friends, a car, health insurance, a good profession, a home. I have my own cell phone to call anyone any time. I am free to make decisions, to go on vacations, to hang out with family and friends whenever I wish. I get to see the sun shine, and I get to choose to have water next to me wherever I go, whenever I want. I love water! I am so free!

So many are still enslaved. According to the US State Department Trafficking in Persons Report 2017, victims originate from almost every region of the world. The top three countries of origin of federally identified victims in 2016 were the UNITED STATES, Mexico, and the Philippines.[7]

Periodicals, statistical reports, and media state that virtually every county within every state in the United States has trafficking.

---

[7] "Trafficking in Persons Report," Department of State, United States of America June 2017, https://www.state.gov/documents/organization/271339.pdf [7/18/2018]

Please, if you do not understand this, research for yourself. Find out what YOU can do to help. The combination of being educated and keeping your senses aware could save a life!

Do you hate what is truly vile? May your heart be stricken with grief for the estimated 20 to 30 million people trapped in this slavery worldwide. May a fire be lit under your feet to do something about it! Please pray diligently for their freedom!

FAITH REDEFINED

God intentionally gives us chapters in the Bible like Hebrews 11, which call our attention to the fact that those mentioned were all incredible men and women of faith. Yet, we read towards the end of the chapter about the OTHERS. Nobody likes to think about the others.

> There were others who were tortured...Some faced jeers and flogging, and even chains and imprisonment. They were put to death by stoning; they were sawed in two; they were killed by the sword. They went about in sheepskins and goatskins, destitute, persecuted and mistreated...<u>and the world was not worthy of them</u>. They wandered in deserts and mountains, living in caves and in

holes in the ground. These were all commended for their faith, yet none of them received what had been promised, since God had planned something better for us so that only together with us would they be made perfect. Hebrews 11:35b-40

The ones labeled as the "others" did not see the answers to their prayers, nor the fulfillment of promise. Good things were not withheld from them because they lacked faith. In fact, they were equally commended for their faith! Even more so, as we read that these who suffered greatly were ones of whom, "the world was not worthy." Notice that they are not named. Forgotten ones, forgotten by the world, but remembered and honored by the Creator of all humankind.

Let us dig in deeper to this. Hopefully, you will be challenged to ask the Lord where you may have errors in your beliefs about faith, just as He challenges me regularly.

I once asked for unshakeable faith. It is not what I envisioned it to be. I thought it meant that I would never doubt the answer to a request offered in prayer, but I doubt many times when I ask for something. I never doubt that He can. I frequently doubt that He will.

So, when I cried out to the Lord after much suffering during an illness one time and I asked Him, "Where is that unshakeable faith that all this suffering is supposed to produce? I am worse than ever in my doubts!"

I heard the Lord clearly speak to my heart, "You **do** have unshakeable faith, Kelly." (long pause to get my full attention). "Whether I heal you or not, you believe in Me, and through all the things you have suffered, you have not turned away from Me. That is unshakeable faith!"

Wow! And I mean WOW!!!! God was right. Imagine that, the God of the universe Who created all things, was speaking to me and He was right! I do not blame you if you inserted "duh" here while reading this. I had my definition of unshakeable faith incorrect and misunderstood.

God was redefining unshakeable faith to me. It is being under fire, under trial, under persecution, in a desert, suffering—and yet never bending a knee to satan. It is serving the Lord no matter what! It is walking as Job did, as Joseph did, as all the disciples did. That is unshakeable faith! It is throughout the Bible, yet I had missed it. I began to rejoice that day when my eyes were opened to this understanding. I laughed and worshipped in the middle of my illness because I had unshakeable faith in the eyes of our Lord!

God redefined my understanding of what unshakeable faith is. It is God, shaking all that can be shaken and what remains is pure faith in Him. It is not in what He will do, not in what may or may not change, not in healing, not in wealth, not in luxury. It is only faith in Him, no matter what!

I doubted my humanness, my selfishness, my ability to ask or desire what God had purposed for me. Doubting our flesh or our humanity is not the same as doubting God. That is because I fully understand how human and fleshly I am. We are all easily mislead. We often pray according to what will ease our pain, what will comfort us, what we want, what we think we need, etc.

I have personal testimonies to supernatural healings in my own body that were NOT remotely dependent upon my faith. I will share a comparison here to help bring an illustration of what I am trying to convey.

There was a time of great illness in my life where I had all the faith in the world that God would heal me when people prayed over me right then and there. In fact, I was 100% convinced of it, and yet, He did not heal me then. In fact, I got much worse and remained ill for several months. What was wrong here? My faith was not lacking, but it was misplaced. My faith was hung up in the outcome of an expected physical healing.

On another occasion, however, I had mega doubt that God would heal me of a severe issue with my spine. I had two MRI's, which showed degenerative arthritis throughout it. One Sunday, little children at church gathered around me and prayed over me. A couple days later, three prayer warriors prayed over me as well. While in prayer, I "saw" a clear shield being placed on my entire back. My assumption was that this shield was holding things together until the doctor could perform another surgery. Prior to this, I already had surgery to correct an area of my spine that had been injured and it seemed evident that there were more injured or degenerated disks which needed repair. This time, to my surprise, the MRI showed little to no arthritis or degeneration in my spine. I believe this was indeed a miracle. My faith was not "up to par;" it was not even showing up on a scale that could be measured. Yet, God, in His infinite mercy, chose to heal me.

I cannot assume to understand why He sometimes heals and why He sometimes does not. I also do not understand why He allows the things He does. I know He does not turn away. I know He is not blind.

Understand, I am not saying that it is God's desire for anyone to be abused, trafficked, humiliated, sold, or tortured. I never want to confuse the evil mankind does to one another to be the desire or will of God—but does God stop it? God does not mind if we wrestle with Him to gain understanding.

I certainly had to wrestle this out with God. I try not to turn away from misunderstandings with God, His Word, or with people. I attempt to persevere in moving towards them so that I may grow, gain knowledge, and discover truth.

Sometimes this is frightening. It was incredibly frightening to ask the ultimate questions that were burning in me: How could a good God allow me to be groomed, tortured, brutalized, kidnapped, betrayed, and trafficked? How could He? Where was He? Why didn't He intervene sooner? Is He really a God of love? Is God involved with people personally? Does He even know I exist? Is there a God? Why was my life full of brokenness?

I know, that I know, that I know, that He is in charge! Yet it begs us to have to face the painful things in life and bring them to the feet of the Lord for His healing and to face Him with it all. Why, just why?

How real can we get with our understanding of God? I prefer to never run from truth. I was lied to enough! I want no part of it.

One of God's names in Hebrew is El Roi, which literally means "the God Who sees me." This is super intimate. Super comforting. Super disconcerting, depending on your life. To know that God saw the things He saw, the things He sees every nano second of every minute of every day. Knowing this, the very idea that God has seen all the things in my life, is not only horrifying, but recognizing this has caused me so many emotions: anger, anguish, torment, embarrassment, confusion, frustration, sorrow, horror, desperation, etc. In my mind, God had a lot of explaining to do.

Lord, I pray for each one reading this to be able to honestly "wrestle" with You for answers where there are seemingly none to be found. I pray that they will clearly hear Your quiet, but steady, peaceful voice to answer them individually and uniquely, and give each one the persistence to not quit asking until they receive personally from You.

WHERE WAS GOD?

As a survivor of nearly every form of sexual abuse and sexual slavery, I had some big issues with God. If God is omnipresent (everywhere all at once), omnipotent (all powerful), and omniscient (all knowing); then why would He turn His back on me? Where was He? Did He close His eyes? Was I blacklisted?

As I mentioned previously, I am not one to shy away from things I do not understand. I came to a place in my healing journey where I desperately wanted some answers from God. I had hit a place of anger at God that was frightening. It was frightening to me for several reasons. One of them being the fact that anger was an emotion I kept in check at all times. In fact, the very feeling of anger scared me. I believed that letting out all the rage that was inside of me would be unstoppable, and that I might never come back to sanity. Yet, I felt this growing, boiling anger inside, like a teapot about to whistle, but it was sealed shut and about to explode instead!

I remember the session that removed most of my anger and began to answer some questions for me. Hopefully, you will take away something positive from what happened for me on this particular day. My answers are not the same answers that you need, as we are all made uniquely.

I had come for inner healing with that anger growing inside and the strong stance that there was nothing God could possibly say or do to answer why He, as a loving God, would stand by and allow such awful things to happen to me. I could not conceive of anything that would silence the growing questions in my head.

The strongest memory at the time was, once again, that first gang rape at age thirteen. The ones working with me asked God to take me back in my memories where He wanted to minister to me. I "saw" the memory of lying on the bed after they were done with me and I had these terrible cuts on my back and my wrists, with scratches and bruises everywhere. I was a bruised and bloody mess lying there. I began to relive the pain of that memory when I "saw" Jesus come to me and begin dipping a rag in a bowl next to the bed and washing my wounds. My first thought was, "what good is that going to do?" I looked and saw that the rag was red with blood, but not my blood. It was His blood running down His arms from the wounds on His face, His arms, His chest, the crown of thorns, and His hands. It was His blood that He was washing me with! As He did that, I had this sensation of pain, both physical and emotional, leaving me and going to Him. I was seeing and experiencing a scripture come to life that I could never fully understand before this moment, "But He was pierced for our transgressions, He was crushed for our iniquities; the punishment that brought us peace was on Him, and by His wounds we are healed" (Isaiah 53:5).

It may also surprise you to know that besides many personal healing sessions to walk me through my issues with God, I also found incredible healing within the scriptures of the Bible. For instance, let me share with you God's view of rape.

> If out in the country a man happens to meet a young woman pledged to be married and rapes her, only the man who has done this shall die. Do nothing to the woman; she has committed no sin deserving death. This case is like that of someone who attacks and murders a neighbor, for the man found the young woman out in the country, and though the betrothed woman scream-ed, there was no one to rescue her. Deuteronomy 22: 25-27

In this passage, God makes it very clear that rape is just as heinous as murder and is therefore just as deserving of the death penalty.

God intentionally honored Rahab, who was a prostitute, because of her obedience. The Israelites laid siege to the city of Jericho. The city was completely destroyed, and every man, woman, and child in it was killed. Only Rahab and her family were spared because she had helped hide the Israelite spies that had come in ahead of the battle (see Joshua 2-6). Afterwards, Rahab married Salmon, an Israelite from the tribe of Judah. Her son was Boaz who became the husband of Ruth. Joseph, the earthly father of Jesus, is her direct descendant. What higher honor could be given by God than to be named in the lineage of His beloved Son, Jesus Christ?! Was she a prostitute of her own will or was she prostituted? Only God knows. I look forward to meeting her one day.

One of my favorite people in the Bible is Joseph. The details of his life can be found in Genesis 37-50. His life is one that I relate to in so many ways. He went from one awful situation to another for many years. His own brothers took him from his parents and threw him in a pit. He was sold as property and became a slave, then he was falsely accused of sexual misconduct and was thrown into prison for several years. Yet in the end, Joseph said a phrase to his brothers that I have adopted as my own, "What you have meant for evil, God has used for good that the lives of many might be saved" (Genesis 50:20).

When you begin to read the Bible with new eyes, you see a trend, which is that the people God raised up and depended upon the most were the very same ones who also suffered greatly. There is a strength of character that builds in one who has suffered. There is also a compassion and empathy that is second to none. I have heard it said that the greater the suffering, the greater the call. This certainly appears to be true in many cases.

What I know to be true is that my suffering has shaped me into who I am today. So, if you like who I am, then you will see this as a good thing if you do not, I cannot help you there.

I have a friend, Aleah, who has been struck by lightning, not once, but TWICE! Aleah had already suffered many tough things in her life. After the first time of being struck, she began to experience some annoying issues with electronics. She would short them out by simply touching them. However, the second time she was struck by lightning, she even destroyed larger electrical items such as stoves and refrigerators.

If you were hit by lightning even one time, you might begin to question what you had done wrong. After the second one, many would question if they were cursed or wonder if God was after them! Not Aleah! She has been a splendid example to many as to how to respond to suffering. Aleah first proclaimed how fortunate she was to have survived. She had this amazing attitude. She would tell the story with laughter. Aleah saw this experience as a testimony to God's goodness! That's right! Goodness! She was not immediately aware, but the truth came out later via neurologist exams that the lightning strikes actually helped reboot her brain like a computer, which helped her with Gulf War Syndrome, as she had previously been deployed during Desert Storm and Desert Shield! This is such a good example of being thankful **before** we have seen the answer.

So, where was God for me? My conclusion is that He was with me every step of the way. He cried with me and for me. He has given free will to all of humankind, not just the good people. Therefore, those whose intentions are selfish and vile have just as much free will to choose what they will do as good people do. The unfortunate consequence of free will is that some will choose evil and perpetrate their evil on others.

God was looking at my future. God is not bound by time. He saw that I would survive and that I would live the life I am living and that I would be involved in the lives of others that He wanted me to influence.

If you have questions in your life about where God was during certain events in your life, I pray that you find your answers by spending intimate time getting to know who God really is. Lord of the Universe, I pray that you would meet each one exactly where they are at and make Yourself known to them.

UNDENIABLE

After understanding God's position in my life, denial as my friend was soon to come to a crashing halt! Life has a way of throwing you some big surprises.

My husband had been somewhat prepared for what was about to be fully exposed. When he was a teen, he had a dream that he rescued a young woman from a brothel. The dream seemed so real to him, like a prophecy. It had put a rescuer mission in his heart; however, once we met and married, he dismissed that dream as being something from a weird teenage mindset. After all, that certainly had nothing to do with my life. At that time, I was a church secretary, came from a normal family, and was living a normal life.

After several years of marriage, I began having memories of a part of my life that I could not accept and refused to believe. I shared them with my husband, David, but then quickly tucked them away. He was convinced these memories were real. Occasionally, he would speak to me while I was mostly asleep, which is when my guard is down and I am the most pliable.

I would tell him details of that life, but the next day, I would not remember having a conversation with him. In the night, I told David one of the stage names I had used, as well as the stage name of someone else, the names of films, the locations, etc. He would try to discuss them with me the next day and I would again dismiss them as fantasy.

Try as I may, that was not a satisfactory answer for me since it was making me miserable. Denial was my go-to for everything. Denial was my protection, my survival tool, my way to face myself and life. I always referred to that particular time frame in my life as the "drug years." So much of it was hazy due to alcohol and drugs. I did recreational drugs to blunt the pain of my other life. I knew I was drowning pain in the drugs but could not face what it was that I was trying so hard to drown out.

One day shortly after one of my facets gave that specific information to David in the night, I was contacted by someone who had made films with me. To protect his identity, I will refer to him as Len. Len referenced the same stage names, the names of films, locations, and all that I had told David previously. I was shocked!

Len spoke of this ring run by wealthy business men who never used their real names. He talked of how they fed me drugs like candy. He witnessed them watching my every move and not allowing me to interact with others. Len saw them bring me in and usher me out when done filming. Initially he had thought it was because I was the "pro" in these films. This was horrifying to hear! It was even more horrifying to face. However, Len said he later began to recognize that something seemed amiss.

My giant fortress of denial came crashing down! There was nowhere to hide from this MOUNTAIN of facts. The truth had to be fully faced, fully felt, and fully dealt with. I was a mess, a pile of rubble, and I did not want to face it. If only there was a way to turn my back on it all. Just look the other way and keep walking like I had always done before. Pretending this was not really my past and that it was merely a shadow of someone I once knew seemed like the best idea. If only the past and God would leave me alone and allow me this one luxury.

Denying the mountain

I wanted to keep my denial. It was comfortable. Facing the full true picture along with every detail is something incredibly difficult to explain to someone else. The loud sobbing, the shame, the terror, the concerns as to what else I was living in denial of—it felt endless! Much was exposed in our brief conversations. So much. Almost too much. I then had to make some decisions.

Do I tell anyone else, besides my husband? Who would I tell? How much would I tell? My family could sense that I was not doing okay. I could not sit on this secret any longer. It was making me physically ill. Frankly, despite all the trauma I was feeling, I could not quit thinking about the battle still raging out there! People are still being trafficked. Sitting quietly on this was not an option for me. It could be an option for others, just not a road I would take. My husband and I both knew that from the beginning.

Standing with me at every moment, David states repeatedly how proud he is of me. He frequently says that I amaze him because I am so sane. His reassurance and love are like towers of refuge in my life. God has given me a companion up to the task and willing to be a living physical representation of how God feels about me. This is no minor thing! If I could give one gift to every survivor, it would be for God to pair them with someone like my David. Can you imagine this—with every new piece of information, with every step I took out of denial, my David loved me more and more, not less!?

Little by little, we carefully shared with our children and other family members first, along with a couple of close friends. The acceptance and compassion I received gave me the courage I needed to move fully out of denial. It was time to own my past. Not to own the responsibility of it, because that definitely belonged to others, but rather, to own its reality.

Approximately twelve years prior to this encounter with the person from my past, the Lord had spoken to my heart that someone who had abused me would one day ask me for forgiveness. I had given up on that ever happening and decided that it must have been my own longing and not the voice of God. The unimaginable now was happening!

Len asked, "Were you forced to do those films or were you paid like we were?"

"Yes, I was forced" my heart pounding in my ears "and no, I was not paid."

Len was clearly disturbed and stated three times, "Please forgive me for being used to abuse you."

I had to stop and think about what was happening in this situation. Embracing the fact that if I forgave Len, I could no longer live in denial. This became an incredibly complicated, life changing moment. Furthermore, there was the realization that I was being recognized as a victim, an unwilling participant by someone who was there! It felt like forever for me to fully grasp all that was happening in this momentary event.

I regained my focus on the request and responded to Len, "yes, I do forgive you."

Len did not try to excuse his personal involvement whatsoever. He shared that he did not fully understand what was happening back then but began catching on during our last film. He quit participating in all films shortly after that. With all the resources on human trafficking available now, Len began to see the big picture, and he had entered therapy as well.

Len explained that he had never been able to live a normal life and had worried about me all these years. Stable relationships had alluded him and he had never been to church. He mentioned that his guilt made him feel as though he was not worthy of God. That life had nearly destroyed him, and he was not even forced into it.

Because I chose to forgive him. He cried. I cried. We were each crying years of tears, tears of relief, tears of pain, tears that had been buried for far too long. Within just a few weeks, Len found a new relationship with God and he began attending church. He was able to finally move on. We can never underestimate the power of forgiveness in someone's life! When we had our last conversation, Len said that my forgiving him gave him the ability to forgive himself. His fiancé said he became a different person, a truly godly man.

Only a few short months later, his fiancé contacted my husband, David, to give him the news that Len had been killed in a car accident. My husband then relayed this to me. I wept, not because of his death, but because of the timing and mercy of the Lord (though I felt incredibly sad for his fiancé)!

It is not a coincidence that he found me just after I was remembering the same details which he was able to confirm with great clarity. It is not a coincidence that I received that desperately longed-for apology. It is not a coincidence that he found a relationship with Jesus just in time—before meeting Him face to face! No one can convince me that this was not divinely timed by a loving and merciful God, a God who does not judge as the world judges, but who looks at the heart.

Now the work within me had begun to go much deeper. So much healing, dealing, reeling, feeling. This was not going to be easy, quick, or enjoyable. Walking away from my constant companion, denial, was not going to be an easy choice. I had to choose not to allow denial to run my life ever again. Denial held such a huge place in my life that not giving in to it is a work even to this day.

Much had to be faced, things too ugly to describe, and I had to get used to accepting the truth. **The truth is that I am a survivor** of the commercial sex industry. I am a survivor of sex trafficking. I've stated this before, but I feel a need to reiterate that I was NOT a prostitute. I was prostitut_ed_. I was a slave. I was used, abused, tortured, beaten, mind controlled, held captive, drugged, raped over and over, betrayed, sold, and nearly destroyed—and yet, despite it all, I SURVIVED!

I am a one percenter! I am a miracle! Statistically, approximately only one percent of sex trafficking victims survive. I am here for a reason. I am meant to be here. There is a plan for my life and I intend to fulfill my destiny.

Lord, I pray for all reading this who have inadvertently participated by viewing pornography in any form. I ask that You help them to find freedom from its grip on their life and that they would experience Your full forgiveness. I ask that each one would become warriors for freeing those who are slaves in the sex trade, whether on their knees warring in prayer or out in the field fighting this battle.

WHY FLASHBACKS?

My journey of dealing with my past began when I was struggling with trusting God in a particular situation and I went for a drive. I was crying out to the Lord and asking Him to please help me understand why I did not trust Him. I easily slip into survival mode when situations evoked stress, anxiety, or any negative emotion. On this evening, I found myself moving into that mode knowing it was not right. In fact, I found myself crying out to God asking, "Why don't I trust you enough to stay out of survival mode?!"

Later that evening we were at church. The pastor stopped in the middle of his message and said, "There is someone here who is in survival mode. You do not trust God and you need to find out why." He then continued his sermon. I was livid! Why would God point this out to me in such a way and then not give me an answer!

In a normal situation, perhaps a person would have felt honored that God picked them out of the audience to speak to that night. Looking back on it, I can see how much God was paying attention to me specifically. I see the love in it *now*... after the fact. But not in that moment. Not at all.

As I went to sleep that night, I begged the Lord to reveal why my "truster" was busted! I did not expect that God would answer that question the very same evening. I awoke in the middle of the night having my very first experience with flashbacks! It absolutely shattered my world! It was full blown Post-Traumatic Stress Disorder (PTSD). Reliving the first gang rape that happened at age thirteen, it felt as if I was there again. This incident is the one detailed in the chapter titled, "Broken but not Destroyed."

With no consciousness of the present, I was back in that moment reliving every detail. I was thrashing and fighting and screaming, "No, stop! Get off of me!" My husband, David, tried reaching over to soothe me thinking he was waking me from a nightmare. Instantly, I reacted by pushing at him and fighting him with everything I could muster. I felt hands all over me, I thought I was being tied down to a bed and was in complete terror! I could not see David. I "saw" them! I "felt" them! I "smelled" them! Very quickly I became violently ill and began to vomit over the side of our bed.

David had to gently calm me down and saying repeatedly, "Kelly, it's me. Honey, you are here with me." Finally, hearing his voice I realized where I was.

These night time intrusions interrupted our sleep for three weeks, and it took several more weeks of me not leaving our house while working through this awful memory. I was nearly agoraphobic during this time, terrified that a flashback could occur at any moment and I did not dare go in public, as they would come on suddenly and seemingly out of nowhere. After going out in public again, certain faces frightened me. Even the slightest resemblance of any of those rapists would cause me to shake and become slightly unhinged. My survival mode was not kicking in and it was horrifying!

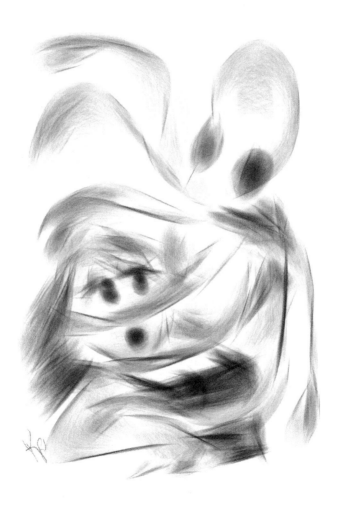

Survival mode felt good, or should I say that actually, it does not FEEL at all. I liked that. I liked not feeling. I still prefer it,

initially. I have walked this road long enough to recognize that it is better to face and feel whatever negative or painful issue I'm avoiding. If I do not, then the poison stays inside, festering. Allowing it to fester underneath is disastrous in the long run. I know from experience that I cannot stay there.

It is my belief that many people could avoid flashbacks if they would trudge forward facing the pain inside rather than trying to bury it. Have you ever tried to hold an inner tube under water? It gets exhausting quickly! It takes much less energy to simply let it emerge and climb onto that thing and ride it out. It is truly the same in undealt-with trauma. The unbelievable effort it takes for our facets to keep something buried or under wraps is arduous work. At some point, something is going to give and then that very thing, that inner tube, will pop up right out from underneath you and dump you right into the thing you were avoiding.

I wish I had caught on to the idea of not going back into survival mode or denial after this experience, but unfortunately, denial was my friend. A friend I had no intention of giving up easily.

Some survivors have kept most of their memories on the surface and never really buried them. Some have deeply buried memories and must go to great lengths to uncover them, while others get the unhappy surprises of flashbacks coming without warning and having their world turned upside down in a moment. Some choose not to remember or face what is buried. Plus, there are those survivors who have a combination of all of these coping skills.

I suppose I fit the combination style of living with these traumatic memories. Having experienced most forms has been helpful in my reaching out to other survivors and understanding their way of dealing... or not dealing. I understand trying to keep it all neatly packaged away and hidden. In fact, I drew a picture representing that frame of mind, which I call "Don't Unwrap This."

This sketch is also a picture of the innocence that should be left "unwrapped" and unsullied by predators. The unwrapping should only occur when the person wrapped in the warmth and safety of personal choice says "yes" by their own free will.

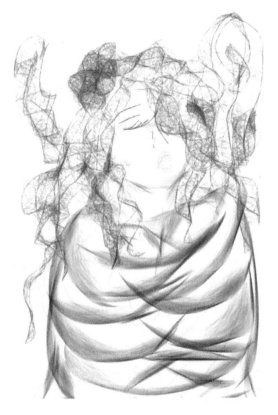

Don't Unwrap This

I have found that a large percentage of survivors seem to have their memories come back piece by piece. As you walk through one incident, another one comes to the surface. This is how it has been for me. For some of us, this is much more tolerable, more survivable.

I also believe it is the way the Creator designed our brains to survive trauma. If we were to keep all of it on the conscious level at all times, we would probably end up as a permanent resident in a psychiatric facility. The ability to compartmentalize traumatic events and the traumatic emotions tied to them, and then to later revisit them as you are ready, is actually a beautiful gift. In fact, having amnesia barriers arranged in place so as not to need to feel and face it all at once can keep you mentally healthy while in the traumatic event(s). I personally am incredibly grateful for this ability. Why unwrap it before you are in a safe place?

There were parts and parcels of memories that were always with me, while others came back progressively, and then there were those that just jumped out of nowhere. At some point, your brain just cannot store anything more in the subconscious and it has to "leak." Leaking is not fun.

I contacted several local agencies to find help, but no one knew what to do with someone who was dealing with an "old" incident. They only worked with incidents that have just been reported recently or within the year. Sadly, this memory was not that old to me. It was as though it had just happened that day. It felt like I was still there, and the pain was very fresh. I had body memories, nightmares, hypervigilance, jumpiness, and emotional melt downs. My husband was so kind, so tender, and probably a little scared.

Our children, who were at various ages of understanding, had to be somewhat informed since it was impossible to hide. We only told the younger ones that I was going through a hard time. The older ones were given more information. One of our older ones cried with me and held me. The younger ones were confused and simply doing their best to just step lightly, speak quietly, and not ask many questions. None of them were accustomed to seeing their mom be anything but tough and always there. It brought some insecurity into the household that was new and uncomfortable for all.

Feeling vulnerable was awful. I was used to being in charge, unemotional, and calm. All these new emotions were frightening for me. A dam had broken. I always used to pride myself in not crying like all the other women. Now I was crying constantly. I also took great pride in being tough. I was even known for being so tough in our local church that someone said, "You can throw anything at Kelly and it bounces off." Much of my toughness was stripped away and I could barely function or leave the house. We had a family to raise, but I needed healing.

Without local help, my only recourse was to seek out information. I found some wonderful Christian materials, which began to help me walk through the emotions and issues surrounding the past abuse. When I use the term, "Christian," I mean it in the sincerest definition of the term as "follower of Christ." I want to acknowledge that there are many who have done horrid things while using the title of being a Christian. Jesus Christ is about love, peace, and unity.

As I began to study these materials, I realized the need to have others to walk through healing with, so I formed a support group. After advertising the support group, the local newspaper called me and asked to do a story on me. They titled it, "Legacy of a Rape." This helped the support group fill up quickly and I was off and running with my first outreach to victims/survivors of sexual abuse and assault. I determined to have it be a place of healing, not just venting.

In His goodness, the Lord gave me an outline for topics. That came to me in a dream one night. I had to write it down as if taking dictation. This is the same outline of topics we still use today at our

Healing Center. I also received training for several types of very in-depth inner healing. These were invaluable tools in the group setting as well as in one-on-one sessions. As the support group continued, I also met with other local advocate agencies.

God does little things that have His supernatural touch involved and you know it is not coincidence! On one such occasion, I heard the Lord speak to my heart nearly audibly, it was so clear. He said, "I want you to write a pamphlet on PTSD that is not Christian based." I was surprised as almost everything I was involved in doing at this time had to do with God. I asked friends and my husband to pray about this. Within the same week, a letter came in the mail from a woman who headed up the sexual assault/abuse portion of our local shelter. She asked me if I would help them write a pamphlet on PTSD. I then realized I had indeed heard God correctly! I was so excited! I helped write the pamphlet for PTSD which is still in use city-wide by several agencies.

I had made a personal decision years ago that whatever I suffered through, I would do my best to use that experience to help others. It adds value to my suffering. One of my favorite passages regarding this ideal is

> Blessed be the God and Father of our Lord Jesus Christ, the Father of mercies and God of all comfort, who comforts us in all our tribulation, that we may be able to comfort those who are in any trouble, with the comfort with which we ourselves are comforted by God. 2 Corinthians 1:3-4

During this same time frame, the mayor and city council gave me an award for "Citizen of the Month" for my work with victims. In addition, I also began speaking in local junior highs, high schools, and colleges about my experience and the road to healing. The bonus to this type of reaching out is that it not only helps others, it is also therapeutic. When we reach out to others, we stop drowning in our own mess. Of course, this was just one of many unveiling moments in my life.

I pray for my survivor brothers and sisters (and those who have suffered any form of abuse) that if you also prefer denial, you will find your way out of it. May you find safe harbor with friends, mentors, peers, counselors, family, churches… just find it somewhere! Please do not stop looking until you find it.

TRIGGERS ARE TOOLS

I may be famous, or infamous, in my area for the following statement: "Blessed are the trigger-makers, for they shall lead us to healing".[8] This statement is probably less appreciated than anything else I have ever said. I say this laughing, because, I nearly hate the truth of it myself! However, the fact is, triggers are a vital tool in God's tool belt. This tool is like a hammer. It is hanging off God's belt, well worn, handy to His grip, always ready, and without any warning whatsoever. BANG! It hits the nail on the head! Of course, if we were given a warning, it would negate its effectiveness.

---

[8] Especially if you have attended a support group I facilitated or have met with me one-on-one.

Triggers come in the form of humans, incidents, objects—like that chair you stubbed your toe on in front of the entire office staff. In the moment, it hurt, and it was embarrassing. How you respond to that incident is a good gauge as to places you may need healing. Would you blame the chair? Would you blame the person who did not put the chair back where it belonged? Would you call yourself clumsy or stupid? Would you run and hide until the redness left your face? Would you laugh because it could have happened to anyone? Each trigger is an opportunity to learn and grow. I am not talking about merely taking your thoughts captive and not allowing them power over you, though that is also a good response to triggers.

Let God get to the root of why stubbing your toe made you feel angry or embarrassed or afraid—it is not about stubbing your toe—It is about what is in your past.

Anyone who has been trafficked knows that our triggers are many, much more than others could possibly understand. The "little things" to the average person can often be monumental to a survivor.

Here is one example from my personal experience. People used to find it funny to scare me by sneaking up on me. I would jump so hard that I would light into the air with my entire body reacting. While for me my first response was horror and shock, to others it appeared humorous. What people did not understand is that it literally hurt my body inside with a type of pain that surged from head to foot. I would often end up with a headache and backache afterwards from jarring so hard. After the initial fear from the moment, anger would begin to burn inside of me. Meanwhile, I would generally try to laugh it off when around others. I initially tried to explain this to my husband when we were first married, but it made no sense to him. It made no sense to me. After all, he was just being playful. We did not understand, because we had not dealt with my past yet.

Another trigger was that I hated surprises. I needed an itinerary of my month in advance. In the porn industry, specifically films, it is rather common place to surprise the victim with unexpected large groups for the film, take her hostage to the scene to be filmed, or fake the death(s) of someone in the room to get her to perform properly. There are also snuff films in which someone is actually killed on set. To my knowledge, I never witnessed that, but I was convinced in one situation that I was in the middle of a mass break-in and shooting, until I saw the cameras. They love to capture real fear on film. Sadly, people viewing these see her as the "star" of the film, when in fact, she is the slave on set. "Please do not set me up with last minute plans," was my plea to all who knew me. I lived by lists of what I would accomplish each day, and one by one crossed off each item. If I had to add an item, it messed me up! Spontaneity was not in my vocabulary. So, who did God pair me with for a husband? Mister Spontaneous himself! Good thing I did not recognize that while we were dating, or I may have run. That surely would have been the greatest mistake of my life!

The reality is, once I began to question this extreme response to something seemingly so insignificant, I began to sense a deeper issue. When I took the time to follow the trail of where these reactions first began, then the floodgates opened to the dozens of memories I had walled off, of being grabbed off the streets, out of theaters, drug out back doors of bars, thrown into cars, and dropped off at unknown locations! Memories flooded of incidents where a surprise was a very bad thing.

My handlers were not kind in the least bit, in fact, they were monsters—this is a huge understatement. They were organized, and they were many. I never knew when or who would be the hand that dealt a blow. Because they crossed several states, new handlers came into the picture all the time. They even surprised me at my regular work locations. I was shocked at the places I was taken and the things I was forced to do. Despite being in a constant state of hypervigilance. It was like living in a cruel paradox, I was never ready for what would come.

The painful and horrifying parts of my past desperately needed healing. Following the trail to the reason why something triggers us is one of the most reliable paths towards healing, as it points us in the precise direction of the source of the wounds. If we were never triggered, we would never seek healing. We would all keep our poison down inside of us and let it rot us from the inside out.

I would like to share an example from someone I was ministering to. We were stuck in her session. She was visibly upset. We could not get anywhere, but she had a lot of fear. While we sat there together, a car backfired directly outside the window of the building. She was instantly startled and was immediately in a memory where her father held a gun to her head! Now we had the memory that needed attention. Her healing that day was incredible. A tormenting memory faded into the past and the truth that she was no longer his prisoner came to the forefront, all because of an outside trigger from the backfiring of a car.

I eventually learned to be grateful for triggers. Well, for the most part. Okay, if I am honest, I only appreciate them after they happen. In the moment, not so much. As a female pastor, I am often confronted with the trigger of male dominance. I must take a moment here and commend the city I live in for being one of the most accepting places of female pastors! However, I still run into the occasional nay-sayer.

Since I had authority figures that were largely male in the trafficking industry, I was very vulnerable to the teachings of some churches as to the inequality of females in ministry. I submitted easily, even though it felt wrong in my spirit. This was before I had any Biblical training and understood little about the original translations of the Bible. Due to this, I took Scripture at face value. I did not know that English was not the original language of the scriptures and is, in fact, extremely inferior to the original texts. It lacks expression, culture, and understanding that was common to its original readers.

I was blessed as I began to grow in the Lord to be surrounded by male teachers who believed in equality. They also understood the depth of the scriptures and the richness of the original texts. They began to train me and show me that women were set free to full equality by Jesus and the Apostles. I could write an entire book on this subject alone, but honestly, I would rather recommend a couple of my favorites: "25 Tough Questions About Women and the Church: Answers from God's Word That Will Set Women Free," by J. Lee Grady and "Why Not Women? A Fresh Look at Scripture on Women in Missions, Ministry, and Leadership," by David Joel Hamilton and Loren Cunningham.

My husband, David, has been one of the greatest tools of God to bring healing into my issues with males. He is very masculine and has no problem with me being the Lead Pastor of our church. He is truly a man's man. Yet, I will never forget the night I awoke to him praying blessings over me and he explained how the Lord told him to acknowledge me as his pastor. He said, "You are my pastor, and I will honor you as such," I was deeply moved, as this brought great healing to me. It was also the support I needed to confirm what I had already felt called to do, but to hear it from my very best friend and husband was that much needed affirmation. Where men had stolen my confidence in my past, David is the gift and tool that God is using to rebuild it in my present.

We love running our home as equals with God as the head of our household. I sometimes have to pinch myself to believe that after all I have gone through, God brought me this beautiful soul mate, a man whose identity is not threatened by equality.

However, with a trafficking past, any authority figure can be a huge trigger. That is why I was always dubbed as "rebellious" when growing up. I despised and held no respect for authority figures, male or female. There is a very good reason that survivors commonly struggle with this. Who do you think affords escort services? It is not generally your middle-income, hard-working class. It is people with power and money, people who rule your communities, your judiciary systems, your entertainment businesses, major business owners, etc. They are people with money to burn and too much time on their hands. While most individuals in law enforcement are upstanding, I have rarely met a survivor who has not had to do things for an unscrupulous officer or two to avoid jail or worse.

Can you imagine why survivors get a bad reputation? The setup is from the beginning to make you behave like an outcast, force you to despise authority, and cause you to have nowhere to turn. It is very intentional. They need you cut off and mistrusting of everyone in any position that might possibly offer you help. You are valuable to them because you are a product that brings in revenue. Whatever it takes to keep that product in line will be done.

I had two police officers who were my main local handlers. They took advantage of that at every chance. Law enforcement officers had been big triggers in my life, triggers that God has used to heal me. I have several family members that are involved in law enforcement and God has used that to help me understand the others, the officers who are honest and have integrity.

However, my first experiences were awful. These two officers were the first ones to initiate me into the ruling class of the city we had moved to when I was 17. They were cruel and perverted. This began a fear of anyone in uniform due to my forced involvement with those two individuals. They did not even try to hide some of their antics when in public, such as trying to untie my shirt in a public restaurant in front of other customers. Nobody said anything; it was as if everyone was as afraid of them as I was.

It felt as though they owned me. They worked for the ring, yet they wore the uniform and the badge which commanded respect from others. Thus, if they said it was okay, then it was not challenged by onlookers. These two had great fun hauling me out of bars or restaurants when I was hanging out with friends just to force me to do whatever it was they wanted on any given evening.

Can you see why a survivor has hundreds of triggers? They really cannot be avoided, so instead, they must be dealt with. When a trigger arises, I try to view it as an opportunity to deal with something locked away or still festering. The healing journey is long and necessary, and it is a journey I intend to stay on until I meet my Creator face to face.

I pray for any survivor brothers or sisters reading this right now. Allow yourself to feel the emotions this evokes: anger, betrayal, fear, hate, paranoia, vulnerability, etc. Lord, I ask that you minister to each painful emotion and any lie that is believed. Guide each one reading this to a place of realization and recognition that You can be trusted with their life. God, speak to their heart right now in a very personal way that comforts the need to feel protected by You.

SURVIVOR SISTERS' DIALOGUE

Meeting my first trafficking survivor in person was something I longed for. I wanted to meet another person, face to face, who had experienced what I had, to talk as openly as possible and to discover what we had in common, or if we had anything in common. I longed for a dialogue that would validate the things I had been through; someone who would understand me in a way that others would never fully be able to.

At the same time, I had the fear of the first meeting of someone with my history. What if she was nothing like me? What if she did not like me? What if our experiences were so different that we would not be able to relate? What if some of what I went through was unique to me and she would not have a clue as to what I was talking about?

There was a desperation to be understood on a level that I can hardly describe. The longing was growing in me. I had not yet met a sex trafficking survivor in person, face to face. I wanted to look in her eyes and see if I was in there too. Would the wounds be the same? Would the betrayals be the same? I wondered if we would share similar qualities and ideals. Would I like her? Would she like me?

I had the experience of visiting with several beautiful survivor sisters online and via Skype. It was wonderful and fulfilling! I learned so much from each of them, yet I somehow knew that the actual physical meeting of another survivor would be life-changing. I sensed that something would grow out of that experience. What that would be, I had no idea. I just knew it could not happen soon enough!

Finally, one day, I met Sally. She had never met another survivor in person either. It was a first for both of us and will forever be monumental! It was a beautiful experience. I could go into it in great detail, but honestly, the following communication between us says it all.

The following dialogue was born out of a set of thoughts that I first sent to Sally and she responded between the lines in such a way as to continue our correspondence, making it into a poetry of two people in one literary art experience. I have certainly never felt inspired to do that before, nor had she.

It left us both very moved, and we hope that it will touch you as well. We took this picture of our hands together that day to commemorate our first meeting.

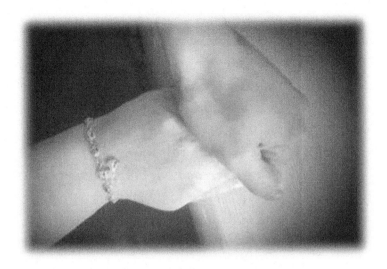

Sally's hand on mine

Survivor Sisters' Dialogue
Written by *Kelly Patterson* & Sally Richardson[9]

We met face to face...
Not a word was spoken.
Both of us meeting our first survivor sister.
Not a word was spoken with the initial shock.

Looking into each other's eyes, with the depth of knowledge and an intensity that only you can understand.
Volumes of knowledge could never memorialize the depths of compassion and understanding with the smallest of gestures.
You get me. I get you. So much doesn't even need spoken. It's understood.
With mutual perception-acceptance is second nature...

---

[9] Sally Richardson is a Survivor, Speaker, Abolitionist, Founder of www.Fighting AgainstTrafficking.Org

We watched one another order from the menu carefully, safely...
Watching for foods that may trigger issues, textures being very important. Safely ordering our drinks (Coffee for you, Coke for me), in case something needs washed down and dissolved quickly so as to not gag either of us at the table.
Presence of safety, while we observed one another... Keeping demons at bay while we cared for the other.
We spoke of it briefly. Amazed at our mutual issues with food.
Softly we spoke of similar elicit nourishment-alarmed by the after-effects, still today and here after...

We shared a tiny piece of our stories decades apart, and yet the tricks have not changed their fetishes or desires. Same filthy beings.
Snippets of our trauma we shared—days upon weeks, months upon years... The realization of identical impurity and fears. These foul immoral corrupt souls.
We spoke some more, this time in tears, astonished that we share the same scenarios, the same degradation, the same beatings and torture.
The tribulation of torment was beyond that of a twinge. Our suffering appears this day staining our affliction-ridden face.

We hugged and didn't want to let go. Meeting let us know we would be forever connected and understood.
Tightly embracing with arms of dignity and grace, all was not lost in our history of self-hate...
Our differences don't matter at all whether politics, religion, race, personality, or age. It's our similarities that count.
Political correctness is not our primary priority but, instead our parallel comparisons...
They make us forever sisters. We survived the unsurvivable.
Which makes us endlessly and everlasting sisters-for our undying perseverance.

TSUNAMIS

Have you ever felt like you were drowning and there was no life boat available? What is one to do in this case? Where do we turn? If there is no life boat, then anything will do—a raft, an old piece of wood, anything to hold onto! Life can be like that. In desperation, we will grasp at anything to keep us "afloat." Unfortunately, many times the things we grab onto are unable to keep our heads above water.

Grabbing onto drug or alcohol addictions, hobbies, unhealthy people, material possessions, status, religion, or even a career will not keep your head above water when the tides come in, or especially when a tsunami engulfs you.

With my past, I just wanted to believe that all suffering in life should be done with. I had been through enough! It seemed unfair to me that I should have to continue to suffer anything else in this life. Life had already been "unfair" to me! I felt it was way past time for my ship to come in. After all, had I not done my time?

Isaiah spells out a truth that is vital to know and understand.

> When you pass through the waters, I will be with you; and when you pass through the rivers, they will not sweep over you. When you walk through the fire, you will not be burned; the flames will not set you ablaze. Isaiah 43:2

It does not say you will not pass through floods, tsunamis, tornadoes, fires, health issues, financial issues, relationship issues, etc. Instead this passage says you will not do it alone and it will not destroy you.

I am not a person to wallow in self-pity, so I did not allow myself to entertain the thoughts of how unfair my life was for more than a few moments for most of my adult life. I was beginning to realize that I needed to actually feel some of this loss, but I did not know how. We have already established the fact that FEELING things is not my strong suit. It nearly always takes an act of God to get me to a place of feeling.

Thus began a several-year season of a variety of different major health issues, health issues that would literally fill a book all on their own. I have often thought of starting a health diagnosis site for weird symptoms just based on my own experiences! When I would eventually come out of one health issue and just barely get my head above water to take a breath, then another one would hit. I was living in one tsunami after another!

During these bouts of health issues, I learned several things about God, about myself, and about the unseen world around us. There are things that simply cannot be explained as coincidence. I am going to share a few of these with you. You can choose to believe them, discount them, or gain from them. It is entirely up to you.

Why am I including this issue in a book that is largely set around trafficking and its effects? There are several reasons, such as the fact that most survivors have major health issues. Much study is being done on this subject. Many of us battle autoimmune disorders, joint issues, and frankly, such an extensive list that I cannot possibly talk about them all.

Several of my bizarre health issues triggered me into memories that I needed to face. I have found this to be a common tool in the lives of many survivors that I have spoken with. As I stated earlier, while I do not appreciate triggers at the time they occur, this tool has been greatly used to change my life for the better.

As a young child, I remember being referred to as sickly. I just seemed to catch everything anyone had. Whatever I caught, I seemed to get it doubly bad. Today we know that physical and emotional trauma greatly affect the body, but that was largely unknown when I was young. Even if it had been understood or taught about, no one around me would have known the origin. I certainly was not telling!

I continued a life of "sickliness," but never anything lasting or too major that could not be explained away; however, once I got into my early 30's, things began to fall apart physically. Each physical issue would bring out yet another trauma that I needed to face. Even still, I could pick up and continue on.

That is, until the "tsunami season" hit me! A few years ago, I began to have ailments that were debilitating. It began with severe migraines, generally four out of seven days per week. I saw specialists, pain management, chiropractors, and neurologists. They decided to layer pain medications in the same way they do for cancer patients. There was nothing more they could do for me.

One of the doctors told me that they had measured pain neurons of a person being shot in the foot and compared them to the pain neurons of a person with a migraine and found that the migraine produced 100 times the amount of pain neurons!

If you have ever had a migraine, you know that the next day is like being hung over, so this essentially left me useless every day of every week. After over two years of these, I could no longer see a purpose for my life. I cried out to God, "Why keep me alive?" I had children and a husband at home that I could not enjoy. It felt so unfair!

On two separate occasions during the migraine season of my life, I had supernatural encounters with God that I will never forget. They were life changing for me. At that time, our youngest daughter was approximately six years old. While I was lying in bed with yet another migraine, tears rolling down my face, I sensed someone in the room. I looked over and here was our little girl kneeling on a chair next to the bed with a tiny picture of Jesus in a frame she had found and placed in front of her. In her sweet faith, she knelt there and prayed. I immediately "left" this dimension. I cannot tell you if it was a dream or a vision, but I was no longer here. I was sent back in time to the evening of the day Christ had been crucified.

I was dressed in the attire of the times along with many others sitting in a circle warming up by a fire outside. Someone asked the rest of us, "Did anyone here know Him?" Everyone was responding that they did not know Him, but had heard of Him, until one woman said, "I knew Him".

We all begged her to tell us about Him, this Man who had been crucified. She began to speak with so much love and admiration for Him that it was contagious. She shared that when He looked into your eyes, you felt fully loved and fully known. She said He could read your thoughts and looked into her soul, but when He did, He delivered love through his eyes. She shared that when He spoke, He was so kind and so wise that she just wanted to listen to Him all day. She said everything that He did or said was filled with compassion and mercy. She went on and on, and the longer she spoke, the more the entire group of us began to weep and wail. We were all weeping because we did not know Him the way that she did. We had missed out!

I was "awakened" or "brought back" by my daughter saying, "Mommy, are you okay?" She heard me sobbing. I assured her that I was fine. Amazingly, that migraine was gone! Never had these migraines ever just disappeared like that. I was left with the most intense desire to know Jesus deeper! That hunger to know Him better has never left me and is my life-long pursuit.

On another occasion where I had a horrific migraine, my husband sat next to me and laid hands upon my head and began to pray. Once again, I "left." Whether it was a dream or a vision, I do not know. This time I was lifted through the clouds and onto a path leading into the Heavenly City. It was so bright, I could hardly look directly at the city for a moment. It was the whitest white I have ever seen. Honestly, I should say it is the whitest white I have NEVER seen on this earth! There is nothing like it.

As I got closer to the city, I began to realize that Jesus would be inside and the excitement in me grew exponentially! I had such an urge to run as I could not wait to jump into His arms! I felt this love flowing from the city that was enormous.

I made my way through the crowds, as I somehow knew He would be in the center, then the moment came. I saw Him! He was reclining in a lounge chair like one would suntan in. This meant a great deal to me personally as it is my most favorite way to relax! I love to lay out in the sun in a lounge chair and just really rest. There was the Son of God—personally reaching out to me from a place of rest that I would understand—being so approachable! I ran towards Him, but as I got closer, my legs felt heavier; my arms felt heavy, my heart felt heavy. As I saw and felt His holiness, I felt immediate conviction of my own sins and flaws. By the time I reached Jesus, I could no longer hold my head up and I fell upon His chest weeping.

Jesus held me close and stroked my hair. At that very moment, all heaviness fell off me and I felt His healing touch, His cleanliness, His acceptance, and His love! I wanted to stay lying there on His chest forever!

Once again, I was "brought back" by someone, this time my husband, asking if I was okay. While sobbing uncontrollably, I explained that it was because I did not want to come back yet! I did not want to leave His beautiful presence! Again, the miracle occurred in which the migraine was completely gone. This time I was left with the understanding that I am to give my burdens to Him. I was also filled with a deep desire for the day when I will be living where He is eternally! There is no place I long for more.

Later, I was instantly and fully healed from all migraines during a prayer session. In the 14 years since, I have never had another migraine.

TRAIN WRECK

For every possible situation you might find yourself in while being trafficked, such as being pregnant, there are people with fetishes. I was shocked at the number of clientele that wanted to experience being with a pregnant slave. Owning a pregnant stripper/prostitute/pet/escort brought in good money for the traffickers.

When I was pregnant, the trauma to my soul was more than I could bear. The desperate need to protect my unborn child was as strong as any mother would feel! The defeat and horror and what my baby was being put through while I was being abused regularly brought an anguish that is indescribable. I focused continuously on escape. I was constantly trying differing methods of running.

I tried to hide and not show up when summoned at more than one point during this pregnancy. This turned into a nightmarish event of literally being held down on a train track and raped by three of the handlers. They used extra brutality to teach me a lesson. They also told me I would pull this "train", or they would tie me to the track and let a train run over me and my baby. There was no doubt in my mind that they would do that, so I took my punishment and did not resist the next summons or the next. After all, I had already suffered and survived much worse events than these.

I soon recognized the all too familiar symptoms of losing a baby. I lost this little one while actively being trafficked and I was approximately five months along. I was taken to the emergency room and the miscarried baby was inspected by the doctor. I named this little boy, Gerad. I am sorry if it makes people uncomfortable to say this, but the truth is the truth. My baby was literally killed due to violent rapes. They raped my little one right out of me! My heart was so broken. I fell into a deep depression and hopelessness. However, this event was the catalyst that gave me the momentum to make yet another plan—one that would finally help me exit the life.

Many years later in a healing prayer session, I gained full understanding of what had happened to my little ones. My babies were taken from me because of the brutality of a life filled with rape. "Sex trafficking" is just a more palatable phrase for repeated, unrelenting rape.

In that healing session, I also received a deep truth of where my babies are. They are with Jesus and I have no doubt of that. One day I will be reunited with them. The following picture is the bracelet I wear today with six colored stones for my living children and three little diamonds on the angel for the babies I lost due to sexual assault.

The addition of the angel with three diamonds to my mother's bracelet brought great healing to my heart. I no longer feel the need to hide my other babies, nor be ashamed of how they were conceived. They are my little precious ones and I feel the same love for them as I do for my children living on this earth.

My mother's bracelet[10]

Most survivors of sex trafficking have lost children due to miscarriages, forced abortions, murder, kidnapping, reselling of the children, or the children are given to the pimp dad or to the state due to prostitution arrests of the mother. It is a sad road for victims of sex trafficking, bathed in physical, emotional, and psychological pain. I have rarely met a survivor who chose this life!

I pray for anyone reading this who has lost a child. I pray that they will find their way to peace that only You can give, Lord. Please be close to each one. As You hold their tears in your bottle, remember them in a most compassionate way this very day. Give them hope for the day they will be reunited!

---

[10] Photo taken by How Eye See It Photography [2018]

FIGHT, FLIGHT, OR FREEZE

From much of what you have read regarding the extremely violent tactics used to keep me in line, you might have the misconception that I never fought back. While I was a victim of their brutality, I frequently fought until I could fight no more. This included fighting the "clientele" on occasion. Oddly, I was never aware of how vertically challenged I was (five feet two inches). I would battle like I was six foot tall. Unfortunately, the fight often is what excites those with fetishes and even with the average pervert — therefore, it was not always in my best interest.

As a child, and throughout my school years, I was involved in many activities. My body was very physically fit. I spent summers swimming and winters ice skating. I was even a cheerleader. I broke state running records in track practices when I was a short distance runner in my freshman and sophomore year. Jazz ballet was a short hobby, but I enjoyed it and used it in addition to other work outs. Riding bicycles was a regular, long-term hobby that began at the early age of six years old along with hiking. My interests also included piano lessons, which I took for several years. I competed in singing competitions, was a soloist and in duets, plus small choir groups. Watching me in any community we lived in would not have raised red flags for most. I was fiercely independent and daring. Appearances are so deceiving, aren't they? I was truly living a double life.

While in grade school, I took a job on a paper route. I loved having my own money and the sense of responsibility that came with it. I would ride my bike early in the morning when no one else was up. However, my nemesis, a ferocious little Chihuahua, would grab onto my leg and not let go. At first, he frightened me. My mother gave me some great battle advice for this. She taught me that dogs know when you are afraid and not to let him see my fear. Then the dog would either back down or become my friend. She was right. The next time that little monster came at me, I gave him a swift kick from my bike pedal and then growled at him. We became friends soon after that.

This advice from my mother proved to help while I was being trafficked. It built a feeling of invincibility and power in me. No matter how many times I was beaten down or abused, I would get back up. There was growing within me a fight that they could not kill.

I did not just lay down and take it! Giving up was not in my nature. However, I did not always pick the right times to fight, if there is such a thing as a "right" time. For instance, I chose to fight back against a very large gang rape. Being surrounded with men coming at me from all sides, taunting me, holding ropes, spraying things in my face to make me dizzy, chasing me with batons and chains is an adrenalin maker which caused my fight to overcome my freeze or my flight. This fight response got me badly beaten. Fight, flight, or freeze were unpredictable foes. There was no knowing which would take over in what situation. That was out of my control!

I hated the freeze response the most. Nothing from the top of my head down to the bottom of my feet would work; it was as though my limbs were shot full of Novocain and went entirely numb. Yet I could hear my heart beating so loudly and it would not slow down! There were times I truly thought I was going to have a heart attack. Freezing makes you feel even more of a victim, all the more shame, and so much more regret. My freeze response caused me the most mental anguish and the greatest confusion. It was so unpredictable that it would catch me by surprise and nearly put me into shock.

Flight never worked until my eventual escape, but the attempts made me feel that at least I was doing something. Something is so much better than nothing. I was equipped with quick reflexes and fast legs despite my short stature. There were times when I nearly escaped being chased by men much taller than me. That invigorated me to some degree. Yet the incredible beatings and torture for the flight response nearly left me for dead on more than one occasion.

When the fight response would take over, I internally felt the best. However, my body felt the worst. The ugly truth is that I would end up on the raw end of that situation every time. It was truly detestable to me to face the fact that I was unable to tackle a man, even the smaller ones. There was very little success on my part, but

135

some satisfaction as I would clean their skin out from under my nails. Bruises were like a banner that I wore with pride. They were visible reminders that I tried to escape. There was even more sense of accomplishment if I left marks on the attacker(s). Once I had lost the battle, I would concentrate on areas of my body that were bleeding or bruised rather than the ensuing rape. They became sources of mental escape as I focused upon the points of pain on my body.

I knew the outcome was nearly always inevitable as I was outnumbered and outmuscled. In fact, I only recall one situation in junior high where I escaped an attempted rape by three guys my age. I fought, and I ran, and I escaped, but only that one time. Perhaps the outcome of this incident gave me the tenacity to keep fighting in the future.

Our bodies are put together in such unusual ways with so many dynamics and secrets to discover. I did not understand fight, flight, or freeze while I was being groomed or trafficked. It was something that I wanted to be able to control but could not. Not understanding these bodily responses created insecurity and a lack of self-confidence within me. I have since come to better understand what was happening to me back then. Would knowing this information have saved me from any of the violence or slavery? Of course not, but perhaps it would have saved me some of the long healing sessions later in life that I had to walk out to gain my sense of self-worth back.

An article in *Psychology Today* titled "Trauma and the Freeze Response: Good, Bad, or Both?" states the following about these responses.

Accurately or not, if you assess the immediately menacing force as something you potentially have the power to defeat, you go into fight mode. In such instances, the hormones released by your sympathetic nervous system—especially adrenaline—prime you to do battle and, hopefully, triumph over the hostile entity.

Conversely, if you view the antagonistic force as too powerful to overcome, your impulse is to outrun it (and the faster the better). And this, of course, is the flight response, also linked to the instantaneous ramping up of your emergency biochemical supplies—so that, ideally, you can escape from this adversarial power (whether it be human, animal, or some calamity of nature).

So where, in what you perceive as a dire threat, is the totally disabling freeze response? By default, this reaction refers to a situation in which you've concluded (in a matter of seconds—if not milliseconds) that you can neither defeat the frighteningly dangerous opponent confronting you nor safely bolt from it. And ironically, this self-paralyzing response can in the moment be just as adaptive as either valiantly fighting the enemy or, more cautiously, fleeing from it.

Consider situations in which, realistically, there's no way you can defend yourself. You have neither the hormone-assisted strength to respond aggressively to the inimical force nor the anxiety-driven speed to free yourself from it. You feel utterly helpless: neither fight nor flight is viable, and there's no one on the scene to rescue you.

Under such unnerving circumstances, "freezing up" or "numbing out"—in a word, dissociating from the here and now—is about the only and (in various instances), best thing you can do.[11]

This and other articles helped me to understand that my body chemicals were going to respond to what ever thought crossed my brain in that nanosecond of time. There was not time to think it over, consider my options, weigh out the consequences, and then act. Instead, my brain jump-started a response within the chemistry of my body to do or not do whatever it did in each situation.

Perhaps you have had similar experiences with fight, flight, or freeze and you are feeling frustrated over your own response. Just

---

[11] Leon F Seltzer, PhD, "Trauma and the Freeze Response: Good, Bad, or Both?" Psychology Today https://www.Psychology today .com/us/blog/evolution-the-self/201507/trauma-and-the-freeze-response-good-bad-or-both [6/16/2018]

know that you are not alone and that your brain and body made the best possible choice to ensure your survival.

I pray that anyone reading this who felt they responded wrongly in a traumatic situation will find relief in Your arms, dear Lord. Please bring comfort, and peace. Return each one to a place of acceptance and self-confidence.

eX

This was the hardest chapter for me to write. To others, it may seem less traumatizing than many of the things I have survived. It contains extremely intimate pain and embarrassment. I will not use my first husband's name, so I will call him eX. Since many people in my life know who he is and due to the fact that this affects my children from that marriage, I will let you draw your own conclusions from what I share. I am not interested in defaming his character; however, these are some of the facts I remember from our time together. I am leaving out much of the worst of it.

At age 17, after being kicked out of the private boarding school (explained in the chapter titled "Seventeen") and on my very first day of attending public school, I met him. It was not an ordinary meeting. He kept smiling and flirting with me in English class. Only minutes later, as I walked down the hallway and took a seat outside the area nearest the secretary's office, not knowing where else to be, eX came and took a seat beside me.

eX introduced himself and then proceeded to tell me a story that terrified me. He said that he could tell I was a good person, but warned me that people were suspicious of me because they had been preparing for a narc to be attending the high school that very week. eX explained that they had been forewarned that law enforcement was planting someone within the student population to find out who was using and selling drugs. He said that he was very well known in the school and would make sure no one accused me. eX shared that the last person who was accused of being a narc in this city was found hanged and tortured. He "gallantly" offered to take me around to parties and help me become a trusted part of his friends. He assured me that if I would just make certain to partake in the drugs at the parties, no one would suspect me because they all trusted his judgment.

eX was playing into one of my worst nightmares. I needed to make it in this school, so I could graduate. Plus, I had been terribly scarred from being bullied at a previous school already. I could not endure that again. I was afraid, alone, and very needy at this point. I watched closely as he greeted student after student and introduced me to them as his good friend. I believed I had met a knight in shining armor who was saving me from possible mis-identification and certain torment!

This started a very unhealthy relationship for me. In my mind, I needed eX in order to survive here. As though my wish was granted, within a few short days, eX asked me to be his exclusively. I thought I was the luckiest person around. After all, eX wanted me and was keeping me safe. Adding to my belief was the fact that I soon became a welcomed part of the group. I attended party after party with him and all the supposed suspicions of my being a narc were gone. Was any part of his initial story true? I have no way of knowing. I do know that any lie accepted as truth will be acted upon and felt as though it is true. I believed him. Therefore, I gladly received the "rescue" from the perceived threat.

We dated the rest of our senior year, but eX was noticeably unreliable. He would take me to parties and disappear, often leaving me with strangers and in very dangerous situations. Due to the use of many potent street drugs during these "dates," I do not recollect much of what happened on these occasions and yet I remember enough to be horrified.

eX also did several things to test my loyalty (or perhaps my neediness) by shunning me publicly to the degree of making me feel unwanted and ashamed. He would leave me alone with people I did not know and go talk to other females and hang on them, then nearly immediately in the next setting, he would be doting on me and bragging about me being his. When he doted, he knew how to make me feel like the most important and special person in the room. eX used the same tactics that are seen in domestic violence relationships, though he never once physically hit me.

He would build me up, only to tear me down. eX would tell me I was beautiful and in the very same breath tell me I needed to drop a few pounds although I was seriously underweight. I was so emotionally unhealthy and needy that I clung to him in desperation. Looking in my rear-view mirror, so to speak, is very disappointing. I missed all the warning signs. It is incomprehensible to me that I allowed myself to be treated so poorly. I was set up perfectly for this abusive relationship.

Despite the protests of my family and friends, I married eX a few months after we graduated from high school at age 18. When you live with what is called "trauma brain", you do not protect yourself. In fact, you run headlong into more trauma without recognizing the signs ahead of time. This is **not** the same as traumatic brain injury. Trauma brain stems from childhood abuse.

> The hippocampus in the brain is the part that helps process information and lends time and spatial context to memories and events. It then assists the transfer of initial information to the cortex which works to help make sense of the information. However, the hippocampus is vulnerable to stress hormones.
>
> When those hormones reach a high level, such as in ongoing abuse, they suppress the activity of the hippocampus and it loses its ability to function properly. Vital information that would make it possible to differentiate between a real and imagined threat never reaches the cortex and a rational evaluation of the information isn't possible, thus leading to underreacting to real dangers and over-reacting to small triggers.[12]

There are a number of ridiculous situations that a healthy person would have run from in my relationship due to the red flags. Instead, my brain did not register the "danger" and I simply dug my heels in to make the relationship work.

Our honeymoon was anything but romantic and should have sent me running! eX had booked a hotel ahead of time, which was

---

[12] Blue Knot Foundation, (2018) "Impact on the Brain" https://www.blueknot. org.au/Resources/General-Information/Impact-on-brain [5/17/18]

very unlike him. This hotel happened to be the same place where I was forced into porn film production on at least one occasion. There was obvious prostitution going on in the rooms around ours. I was so triggered, all I wanted to do was to lock our door and not leave the room. I was looking forward to a honeymoon when eX presented me with his wedding gift, LSD for each of us. My heart broke.

Like any other young woman, I had dreamed about what my honeymoon would be like. I thought it was to be sweet and romantic. This was not what I had dreamt of! He was so excited about this "gift" that I did not have the heart or the guts to say, "Please, let's not have a psychedelic honeymoon tonight."

Part of trauma brain is not being able to always put things into a sequence of events that are directly related to the trauma. I knew *that shortly after the LSD took effect, eX left me for the weekend and that I had always hated our honeymoon weekend. I also had patchy memories of being taken from that same hotel to a neighboring state. I remembered being behind stage with a very famous rock band and being presented to them as their entertainment after the concert.

Before writing this portion, I decided to search that band's concert dates to be certain I was not mixing up two separate events. Imagine my non-surprise to find evidence on their website that listed a past concert that coincided with my honeymoon weekend in the very same neighboring state. How could he leave me all weekend on what was supposed to be the best night of my life!? I had always been bothered by his absence and was plagued with hatred of our honeymoon. Yet, I could never quite piece the two events together for certain until I checked the concert tour archives.

This was just one of several such times where I was the "entertainment" for famous rock bands. I assume this is one of the many reasons why my handlers nicknamed me, "High Dollar." This nickname was often followed by a derogatory term that I will not give space to. Terms like that put the guilt and blame back on me. I subconsciously took those words inside and begin to believe them. Society needs to understand that throwing around derogatory terms like that must end. You may never know who you are saying it around! What if your words are being used to add to the shaming and victim blaming that someone is currently living under?

As survivors, we often doubt ourselves, our recollections, and even our assessments of how bad it was. We often would find ourselves comparing our stories to that of others and thinking others had it worse. This is all part of the trafficking mind games: mixed messages, doubt, and self-blame are instilled by those handling us. Being in a marriage like I was added to these messages.

Throughout our marriage, eX was absent much of the time. Each time he did not come home when I got off my day job, I would begin to have panic so severe that I would double over in stomach pain and migraines. These stomach issues became so severe that I went through medical testing only to be told that I had a "nervous stomach." What an understatement! I never knew where he was. Did he know where I was? When I could not reach him, I would run towards the bars to find friends! I was terrified to be alone wherever we lived, as my handlers had come into our home and grabbed me on more than one occasion. Sometimes this was successful, but most times it was not any safer than staying home. There was nowhere to run.

eX never worked a job more than a few days at a time during our marriage. In these years of our marriage, he was supposed to be attending a university. However, his grades along with notes from teachers reflected that he was rarely, if ever, in class. Where was eX while I was being trafficked during our marriage? My day jobs only paid our rent, food, and a little extra, and of course my night "job" paid me nothing. When he did show up at home, why did he come home with clothing for me to wear that he had purchased, and on more than one occasion brought me clothing accompanied by another woman who "helped" him pick the clothing out? I was so angry that he had female "friends" with him that I knew nothing about.

How on earth did he always have money for expensive drugs? I wonder about the time he sent me alone to pick up pot from a guy across the street. eX reassured me it would be okay, but I got viciously raped instead. I walked back across the street afterwards with the pot in hand, torn clothing, and a wounded soul. To add to the humiliation and abandonment that I felt, I entered the home to find that nobody was home. Despairingly, I locked the door, sat on the couch wide awake, angry, afraid, and alone in the dark all night. Did eX pay for the pot by selling me? Where was he in this dark hour? Where was he in every dark hour of our relationship?

During the active trafficking years of my life, he often left me alone for days and days at a time. His involvement has not been fully revealed, although I have recovered some memories surrounding this. In fact, on the film sets, others who were there discussed his involvement, but I refused to hear it. Some of his involvement seemed to be more that of complacency, not of actual trafficking. Either he knew, and he did not care, or he knew and was equally afraid of them. Or he was allowing it and receiving some form of payment for "loaning" me to them. I do have some memories where he was actively involved in awful things that happened to me, portions of which I had always remembered the beginning and the end, but nothing in-between until the last few years. Blocked memories are often held in the conscious mind like bookends. It is the "books" in the middle that I needed to get to.

I have so many questions. Was he a willing participant who was receiving payment for allowing me to be used? Or was he himself a victim of his own addictions and ignorant to some extent? He certainly did not live the rich life of a pimp. It is difficult to realize and accept that I may never know the full story of our life together.

For my precious fellow survivors and those who know them, the good news is that trauma brain can be healed. Our brain is a magnificent creation that can form new pathways. With healing, you no longer need to follow the old trails of the past. If you are a survivor, you have already endured more than most could ever live through. You can do this! I pray for your learned skills of pushing through hardship to come out strong and be used to forge a new life in the journey to maneuvering through the new terrain in your brain.

THE ESCAPE

I was determined to leave that life one way or another, alive or dead. A few months after I turned 21, I quit my full-time day job and picked up a temporary higher paying day job. I saved every penny and told my husband (eX) that I wanted to move to the west coast immediately without giving notice to anyone! Since he had talked of moving there previously, it was easy to get him to agree. We moved in temporarily with his parents where we could save an even larger stash of money to move. It also kept me in an environment where I did not have to be alone and was somewhat safer. Shortly after moving in with them, I lost my third baby. It was time to go as I simply could not take any more loss. We moved in May. On our way through Montana, we met up with a guy who wanted to move to the west coast also, so he jumped in with us and off we went.

We arrived at our destination and initially moved into a house full of college students. All of them were drug users. Unfortunately, that was something I also had hoped to escape, but it was right there in the house. Those first few months are somewhat of a blur, and I am uncertain as to why. I do remember that I was determined not to use any drugs once we moved to our west coast destination. However, I am not certain if I totally avoided them or not.

I recall going to a bar on Halloween with eX dressed as I was often dressed in the life, entirely too inappropriate for public. *It is difficult to look back on that time in my life and come to grips with the fact that was me, and that I dressed like that in public!* Shortly after walking into this bar, eX disappeared. That is all I remember of that night. Anything could have happened, and frankly, most likely did. It has been my experience that when I have a partial memory so vivid, but the rest is missing there is usually something devastating that happened. I do not seek to dig up memories as there are far too many events to remember. Memories seem to come up as God brings them to mind so they can be dealt with during a healing session or they leak out when I am unprepared. In either case, I do not go looking. It serves no purpose and I am nearly always blocked when trying to do so.

So many things about living in that realm are nightmarish and surreal. It is quite difficult to explain to someone who has never been there. There is a learned ambivalence that is experienced when you have been involved in something so very horrific and yet so very sexual. Ambivalence involves having mixed feelings or contradictory ideas about something or someone. Regarding trafficking, or in any type of sexual abuse, it could better be defined as feeling both pain and pleasure within the same incident. Ambivalent responses to abuse can be both physical and/or emotional pains and pleasures.

150

This is often missed or misunderstood, even by the victims themselves, that they are being intentionally taught to be double minded. This double mindedness is what causes some of the greatest shame and guilt in one who is being groomed and trained by traffickers. Traffickers generally make certain that there is both the experience of the physical pain of being tortured while also being forced to experience sexual pleasure in the very same time span. Can you understand why this torments the mind and body of the victims of sexual abuse of any kind? Who do you tell? It is this deep shame that also facilitates the near impossibility of a victim being able to ask for help or to tell anyone.

Despite my mental torment, I quickly found a full-time day job at the university in the city we resided in. I would ride the bus daily to and from work. Something I do remember quite well about having that job is that there were two guys on the university campus who were either connected to the original trafficking ring or another similar organization. They immediately began to ride the bus after work with me. On that first bus ride with them, they forced me off the bus at a stop several miles from home. They took me into a building set-up specifically for ritual abuse to remind me "you can never leave."

You are possibly wondering how they could force me off a city bus in public. A better word to explain this would be the term coerced. I had been living under a domination lifestyle since I was a child and I knew nothing different. "No" was never an option; I knew what could happen if I did not comply. I honestly do not know how many times these two specific men followed me and forced me off the bus.

When I would arrive home late from work, eX would ask why I was late. My response was always the excuse of wanting to walk and enjoy the beauty outside, never revealing what was really happening for a few reasons. Facets of me understood their message to "shut up" and understood the consequences far too well if I did not follow the "rules." I did not trust my husband at that time with any information. The most complex reason was that I would disassociate from the extreme trauma. This resulted in me not remembering what had occurred prior to leaving their presence. Therefore, at the time, the excuse of enjoying the scenery seemed true to me due to the complexities of dissociation. Later in life, I came to understand dissociation and its diverse complications. This knowledge has helped me greatly in putting the pieces together of many seemingly disconnected situations.

We eventually moved into our own small communal living arrangement with some other people we met. We began taking in more and more people. We brought in a family with four children as well. Little did I know that this family would be the very people God would use to help me escape the extended clutches of this ring and their associates.

Meanwhile, the two men from the campus started getting more blatant. They would follow me wherever I went. I would be buying groceries just blocks from home and they would follow me up and down the aisles intimidating me by walking up behind me and touching my waist, peeking around aisles and blowing me kisses, making hand gestures that gave the message to me that I belonged to them, and most terrifyingly to me... they would say my name over and over. It would send chills down my spine each time. I would always walk away wondering on the inside how they knew my name. They had done their jobs well by retraumatizing me and keeping me on their invisible leash.

One day they decided to follow me the entire way towards my home, nearly stepping on my heels. I kept walking faster and faster with my heart pounding. They just increased their pace to stay right on me. Fortunately, the father of the family that had moved in with us was outside and noticed what was happening. He sent his children to run towards me calling my name out loud. I had never been happier to see those children! The two guys spun around on the sidewalk and walked back the other direction.

When I arrived in the yard with the children, their father warned me who these guys were and who they were associated with. He told me that our communal group would not allow me to be alone like that anymore and would watch out for me. This Christian family began to talk to the entire commune about Jesus. There was something special in the way this guy talked and shared. He shared things I had never heard before and made Jesus come alive for me.

I recommitted my life to the Lord and this man prayed over me to be filled to overflowing with the Holy Spirit. In that moment, I was immediately brought out of my bondage to the ring, to drugs, to foggy thinking, and into clarity of thought and purpose. It was as though I had a new brain! I was instantaneously different in just about every way. This was a true miracle and I knew it. I gave up everything that was not godly that day and have never looked back.

It was definitely the filling of the Holy Spirit who denied them access to me after this event. Due to this complete transformation, the traffickers were never able to sell or use me again. It ended then and there! I had finally escaped for good and I survived it all!

While my eX made a temporary change in lifestyle while we were still living on the west coast, once we moved back to Heartland USA, he soon fell into old habits of drugs and women. After much counseling and yet another affair, I wised up and filed for divorce. The children and I moved on to a new life!

Starting a new life as a single parent was not easy. I tried dating and found it frustrating. I either trusted too much or not enough in most cases. However, I personally found that being alone was not nearly as lonely as being married to a cheating, absent, non-communicating man who did not have any of the same beliefs or desires in life that I had. God had much better plans for me anyway. I just did not know it yet.

Just like a beautiful butterfly comes out of an ugly cocoon, so too did beautiful children come out of a hideous marriage. Despite all the suffering, I would never change having the butterflies in my life! They are treasures that have brought and continue to bring IMMENSE value to my suffering.

I am reminded of the butterfly's struggle to get out of their cocoon. It is that struggle that makes their wings large and strong enough to carry them through life. Without struggling they would not have strong enough wings to fly to freedom and carry their beauty to the world.

I was also in a cocoon. God indeed makes all things beautiful in His time. I scarcely remember that ugly cocoon. In fact, it is difficult to believe the person written about in this book is me. I am grateful to be flying free.

Join me in praying for the captives to be set free worldwide! Creator of all humankind, please set the slaves free! Send them real help and give them resolve to survive until they have escaped the clutches of those who are harming them.

LOVE CAME FOR ME

I am a deeply spiritual person. I must share what was the biggest key to moving forward, no matter what your past entails and no matter what your beliefs are.

God does not need another human to sit in and help you hear Him; however, sometimes we simply cannot focus enough to do it on our own. Yet other times, the Creator chooses to bypass all we know and get us when we least expect it! For me, that is often in my sleep or right when I am about to go to sleep! He loves to minister to me in my sleep for that very reason. Brilliant of Him, isn't it?! I see it as a sneak attack, one I have learned to value like a great treasure.

As I have referenced earlier, being trafficked and abused caused some significant issues with me and God. My biggest issue was believing He loved me. If you love someone, would you not do everything imaginable to protect them from something as horrendous as what I had lived through? I kept hearing people speak of God's love. I read about it in the Bible. I tried to rehearse the idea in my mind, but nothing could break through the barriers set up on the inside.

I believe there is set within the DNA of every human being a longing for that love, a hunger that nothing else can fulfill. However, if you hunger long enough and are fed nothing but worms, you may choose to turn away either in anger or in pain. After much searching, I had determined that the Creator was indeed real, and that God loved His creation. I was convinced the error in my feelings had something to do with me, not God. Therefore, I chose seeking after this love I kept hearing about. I had no intention of leaving this earth empty handed, no matter how long it took! Surviving my past also put a tenacity in me to not give up! I certainly was not giving up on the very thing I knew that I desperately needed. I needed to know that I was deeply and personally loved by the Creator!

This longing began a several-year commitment on my part to settle for nothing less. I prayed every day, several times a day, "Show me that You love me." I would not stop until I knew that I was loved! I needed more than someone else's say-so. Reading words on a page were not fixing this longing.

Survivors of sex trafficking have already lived through the most horrific things that one can imagine and once we recognize our strength, most of us will find our inner warrior.

One evening as I was lying down to go to bed, I heard beautiful music like chimes come in the wind. It was as though the wind and the chimes were inside my home. It was beautiful and enchanting and completely engulfed me. As I was listening and trying to determine where it was coming from, I heard a voice in the music say, "Kelly." The clear and audible voice was coming from outside of myself; It was clear and audible. I checked to see if eX was awake and had said my name. He was sleeping. I even checked on my children to see if it was one of them, knowing in the logic zone that they were too little to speak that clearly. Of course, they were sleeping, so I went to sleep.

Upon waking the next morning, I could not shake how beautiful that voice was. I was certain it was God, but what was He trying to say? That evening, as I laid down to go to sleep, the same thing happened, identical to the night before, the wind, the chimes, and the voice saying my name! I was in awe, but still did not understand the message.

The next morning, I called my pastor and shared this with him. He asked me if I knew the story of Samuel (see 1 Samuel 3). Since I did not, he shared with me where to look the story up in the Bible and exhorted me to do what Samuel did. In short, Samuel heard God call his name three nights in a row and when Samuel asked his priest (pastor) what to do, he was told that if he heard the voice again, he should say, "Speak, Lord, for your servant is listening."

Since this was my third night, I sat up in bed ready to say the same words, although, I fully intended to be let down. I felt that there was no way God was going to come a third time and speak to ME, but with that seed of hope, I sat there. Only a few minutes passed when I heard the beautiful musical chimes in the wind come through the house! It surrounded me as the voice spoke out of the music and said, "Kelly."

Now I was all prepared to follow the script and ask, "Yes, Lord," but I did not have time to ask or say anything. The Lord just continued saying my name over and over and over and over. He then continued by saying, "Kelly, I love you." He said this over and over and over as well, and finished with, "Do not have fear, I love you." These were not just words, I could FEEL them. The words had life in them, comfort and hugs in them. I felt loved by the Creator for the first time in my entire life! It was liquid love, as though I was swimming in it or surrounded by it, and it has never left me to this day.

I was new to this Christian stuff, especially anything remotely supernatural. As a child, I had seen the movie where Moses heard God's voice and his hair turned white! Assuming this would always occur when you encounter God, I ran quickly to the bathroom mirror to see if my hair and eyebrows had turned white! I am sure that gave the heavenly realm a good laugh!

When I told my pastor the next day, he asked me if I had ever read the scripture, "Perfect love casts out all fear." I had not heard that passage before. Up until this time, I had not been able to sleep at night. Every little bump or noise would frighten me. Not only was I fully convinced of God's love for me from that night forward, but I was also FULLY healed of that fear of the night. God had done a bonus healing!

To this day, no matter what I have been through since then, I have never doubted God's love for me. Knowing that infinite, unconditional, tangible love has gotten me through everything in ways I could not have otherwise. Knowing you are loved by the Creator is life altering in ways I cannot even begin to express! My entire view of this world, of what is fair or unfair, of suffering, of loving others was all changed in a moment! Knowing the Creator loves you helps you love yourself also.

How I wish God would grant this same experience to every individual. I cannot tell you why He allowed me to experience this, but I can tell you that God knows each of us so individually and He knows where and how we are broken. God knew that I would never accept or believe His love for me any other way. In His intimate devotion to us, He will carefully structure the way to Him on a path that is perfectly designed to the specifics of your character, your history, your future, and your needs.

God has NOT stopped being supernatural just because humans have stopped believing that He is!

Lord, I pray for all who are reading this who do not know for certain that they are loved by You. That they will have a supernatural encounter with Your love! Give them the tenacity to ask until they receive.

LEARNING TO LOVE ME

David began to catch on early in our marriage that I had been wounded deeply. I shared a few things from my past, enough to give him the picture of how broken my trust of others was. I was so untrusting that it may have driven another person mad, but not David. He was up for the challenge! He came to me one day and said, "I am so sorry that men have hurt you so badly." He said that he would earn my trust.

I felt instantly guilty and told him I did not feel that was fair to him, as he was not one of the ones who had betrayed me. David's response was, "I am a man and men have hurt you. Please forgive me, as a man, for what men have done to you."

I was stunned. I literally did not know how to respond. I found myself fumbling for the words to say "I forgive you" to a man who had not betrayed me. This was my first introduction to identificational repentance. It truly started me on a path to healing that I could not imagine was possible.

I had been living behind such thick walls that I was not aware of how hurt I really was. I kept all emotions at bay. This man. He was pulling things up out of me! That day has stuck in my memory strongly because I literally was feeling emotions that were unidentifiable. Was it pain? Was it awe? Was it confusion? Was it relief? I was not sure what I was feeling, but I knew I was feeling.

I also wore unknowingly another type of covering. It was not visible to most people. Only the truly discerning could see it. I was dressed in shame.

I made many choices out of my shame and my pain that had long lasting consequences. I cannot pinpoint them really, but shame was this abiding thing that just hung out in the back of my every decision for years. It was an inescapable wrecking ball. Shame taints your perception and steals your vision. Dreams and joy feel too far out of reach when shame has its grip on you.

I can even remember feeling shame for having shame. To recover from shame, we must first acknowledge that we even have shame. So, the very first step is to identify it. The feeling of shame keeps a person in hiding. It is so sinister. Staying hidden or hiding the thing(s) that caused the shame in the first place only adds to the enormity of the issue. Shame somehow infects our thinking like a disease eating away at who we once were and in turn causing us to believe that we are or have become personally flawed or defective in some way.

Shame is also felt when wrongs are done to us—things such as abuse, teasing, bullying, abandonment, being devalued, parent's behaviors towards us, betrayals, etc. It can also be felt by such things as having perceived physical imperfections or living in poverty.

I have personally found shame to be one of the most difficult mountains in my life. Even when I am doing well and feeling good about things, it will sneak up on me out of nowhere and knock me down. I get up much quicker these days compared to when I was younger, and the occasions are much rarer. I credit that to my immense healing, but also to having a loving and faithful husband. He is my best friend and I can trust him. Please do not misunderstand me to say that it takes another human being to fix shame, but it certainly does help. Acceptance is such a healer.

I cannot think of another crime where the victim of the crime carries the shame. The shame should be on the perpetrator(s) only, but that is rarely the case, if ever. For instance, if someone steals your car, it is unlikely that you will be ashamed of the incident. You may feel a bit violated, but you will not carry long lasting shame for this event. You will blame the one who stole your vehicle. If the thief is found, they will be made to pay for their crime. Never once, would you, the victim, face possible jail or scowling looks from others. Rather, you would most likely be comforted, people would shake their heads at the thief, and that would be the end of it.

Unfortunately, in the case of any form of sexual abuse, the shame falls on the victim rather than the perpetrator of the crime. The sad fact is that many victims are met with disdain or disbelief from others around them. I have met so many who tried to tell someone when they were young only to be dismissed. This forces the feelings of shame to burrow deep inside the victim of the crime.

Shame is added by laws that call for the arrest of those who are prostituted. The worst of it is that several things which are of much more value than a vehicle have been stolen! These involve innocence, choice, safety, trust, health, goals, justice, joy, hope, self-worth, relational abilities… and the list goes on.

A major factor in healing from shame comes from a healthy identity in God. No matter how you see yourself, God sees you as valuable. Read Psalms 139 to see how much time and thought God put into fashioning each of us.

We all desperately need healthy human relationships. We must find safe people to be real with and take baby steps to move forward in these relationships in order to slowly build our trust (fix our "busted trusters"). This is where we can find that much needed human acceptance and affirmation. We were created to be relational. Trafficking tried to cut us off from all that is normal to others, to keep us from real relationships and friendships. All this was done to make us dependent upon the traffickers because—as they beat into us daily—we were expendable, worthless, and unwanted. I look back on it now and see the irony in those phrases they used against us because in truth, we were worth a great deal of money and in high demand. We were a commodity they did not want to lose and of great value to their "industry."

Often, we try to trade-off the need of relationship with anger and behaving bristly. We will give off the vibe that we do not need anyone! Anger is not a trade-off for shame, though that is often what we do. The internal thinking on this is, "if I can be angry, then I will not have to feel the pain of the shame."

Shining a light into the dark places where shame resides will dissipate it more and more. Then the dark places become brighter and brighter. Finding a safe person to take those ugly stories of darkness to is paramount to moving forward into the warmth of the light. It is when light shines into the dark and hidden places that sweet release is found. It takes just one safe person to enter our life, and then relief is found, hope is restored, and self-worth begins to grow.

A beautiful promise from the Lord to those who turn to Him with their brokenness is found in Isaiah.

> He has sent Me [Jesus] to heal the brokenhearted, to proclaim freedom for the captives and release from darkness for the prisoners...Instead of your shame, you will receive a double portion, and instead of disgrace, you will rejoice in your inheritance. Isaiah 61:1b, 7b

This inheritance is an eternal thing, not fleeting like the things so easily lost on this earthly plane. Traffickers put so much emphasis on your outward beauty that it is difficult to overcome even after years of healing. We must work to find our internal and our Eternal value. The internal and Eternal value represent beauty that is lasting and will never fade. "Charm is deceptive, and beauty is fleeting; but a woman who fears the Lord is to be praised" (Proverbs 31:20). Using the term "fears" in this passage does a great injustice to the original language of the Bible. This is a Hebrew word יָרֵא (yare) which means morally reverent. In other words, it is a woman who is in awe of the Lord. Yes!

It often takes someone who has been in the life a while to recognize the sacredness of their physical beauty. It takes time to learn how to dress with a certain amount of modesty and yet still be trendy, if you wish. Initially after coming out of the life, I did not even know that I was not always appropriately dressed. I was accustomed to a certain style. It is something that needs to be taught. I still enjoy wearing heels occasionally, but I got rid of the stilettos— much to the relief of my feet!

Do not be too hard on those you see dressing with too much skin showing as you do not know where they have come from, nor do you know where they are going. Something I am keenly aware of everywhere I go is that I never know who is in the room, what they have been through, what they are involved in right now, and where they may end up. We often are guilty of jumping too quickly to judgements based on the outside appearances of others. Meanwhile, the Bible expressly gives us the opposite example "The Lord does not look at the things people look at. People look at the outward appearance, but the Lord looks at the heart" (1 Samuel 16:7b). I love this so much!

When I am faced with individuals that I do not enjoy or understand, I try to remember to ask God to let me see them with His eyes. It is amazing how your perspective of others changes once you are willing to let go of your own perceptions. There is an additional bonus to this, as well. When you see with God's eyes, you are not easily deceived, nor do you walk in the same fear of others that you may have otherwise. His eyes and vision are perfect. It is a truly beautiful experience to behold someone you once looked at with disdain and suddenly you see who they can become or who they are inside! This practice has helped me to be a visionary and an encourager. An unexpected BIG bonus to this is that you also see yourself differently! Yay!

I pray that anyone trapped in the grips of shame will find that one person to begin the trek towards healthy relationships. I also pray that each one will be surrounded by trustworthy and safe individuals to walk out their journey unafraid and unashamed.

THE PENDULUM

Deni Anderson is my wonderful life coach.[13] She is one of the kindest and most intuitive individuals I have ever spoken to. I had a series of events which bordered on stalking and harassment that occurred over a short two-week period. This was causing me to have fear and jumpiness. Over the past couple years, I was in a place of not being stuck in that fear, so it was unnerving finding myself there once again. I was not sure where to turn since an outsider might consider me paranoid if I shared all of this with them.

As God's timing is perfect, I happened to have a preset meeting with Deni. I unloaded all the events of the past two weeks

---

[13] Deni Anderson, Life Coach, Rebecca Bender Initiative, Founder of Justice Plus Freedom

and she began empathizing with me! She assured me those events would have caused anyone to have concerns. Deni just has a way of causing you to think deeper that is difficult to explain to others. She is so in tune with the Holy Spirit that she literally just pauses, listens, and then asks questions which are right on target. She frequently reminds me to ask myself how I would respond to a call from a survivor with the same questions. That helps me to remember to show myself the same understanding and kindness that I would give to another.

As Deni asked questions, an old fear had surfaced regarding the unknown—not knowing who, when, where, or what was going to come against me next. This was a familiar pattern of being trafficked and of being kept on edge. I did not want to be stuck in this place of fear. While I was able to recognize that my God is bigger and always with me, the reality is that dreadful things still happen in life. Deni asked me where I felt the truth of that knowledge in my body. Oddly, I felt it in my eyes and a little in my heart, which immediately helped me identify that I have just seen too much. It felt as though my heart had "butterflies" like one usually gets in their stomach when feeling nervous.

Deni asked me what God would want me to know as a result of seeing too much. I immediately thought about how God sees all and yet He is still God, still holy. It was then that I connected to the fact that we have God inside of us; therefore, His holiness resides within us no matter what we have seen. That is when I realized the deeper part of why I was being so deeply affected by the stalking and harassing. I was feeling slimed, dirty, and controlled because one of the individuals had texted me as though he knew me, but then got flirty and controlling within seconds. I blocked the texts, but I had not blocked the feelings!

Deni asked me, "What would the Lord like to do with those feelings?" As I closed my eyes, I could "see" the slime coming down off me and on to Jesus. I was reminded that this is what He did at the cross; He took it all and is still taking it all on. As the slime went to Him, it instantly dissipated. I understood that I can do this each time I feel this in the future. What a great tool!

Immediately the concern in my mind changed to wondering where had my ability to go numb disappeared to? As I was pondering this, Deni asked me what might my early warning signal be next time, so I do not get pulled down so far? I could not think of one. We discussed my survival mode, my numbing, and my denial at length. I did not want to tip over into victim mode like that ever again.

It was like a pendulum was inside of me swinging too far in either direction. On the one end was victim mode/fear and on the other was denial/numbness. Deni asked me what would the balance look like? I immediately knew it was "facing the truth with peace." Wow! What a revelation. Facing the truth with peace is so opposite of both fear and denial. It is perfect balance. I want to live there!

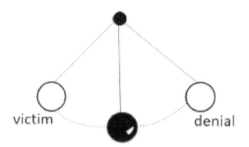

facing truth with peace

As we prayed together, we both saw an early warning signal being put in place. Deni described what she "saw" (which looked just like what I "saw") and she asked me if a big red light on the wall going off with loud constant beeping meant anything to me? Indeed, it did!

My husband and I had once stayed in a hotel across from the Pentagon a couple years prior to this conversation with Deni. David and a friend of ours went to eat that evening and I just wanted to rest in bed. We were staying on the 19th floor, I believe, when a huge alarm on the wall in my room with a rotating red light started going off. I certainly could not miss that noise or that sight! There was no ignoring it! I had thoughts of 9/11 because of my location. I grabbed my phone, purse, and shoes and began to run down flights of stairs. My little legs were ahead of everyone except one of the staff, who was keeping up with me! It turned out not to be anything of significance this time, but the point of this is you cannot ignore a loud red siren on the wall next to you.

I believe God has implemented something in my life that I will not be able to ignore. An early warning signal means you get advanced notice, which means you avoid disaster! Thus, I can face the truth with peace. This was another advancement in healing for my previous unhealthy way of living which was to, "go numb, don't feel, then deal." Truth WITH peace, now that is a much healthier way to live! I can avoid the pendulum swaying out of control by holding onto God while He implements the early warning signal. That has already come in handy a few times since our session.

I pray for balance in all the ways that are out of balance for all who are reading this. Lord, show each one where they need balance and help them attain it.

TEN THOUSAND
I LOVE YOU'S

Sadly, many survivors can never find a mate due to all the betrayal and mistrust they have experienced. It is so difficult when you cannot even trust your own judgement. After all, our previous judgements of people usually ended up in disaster.

After being single-again for a while, I began dating, but I could never find the person who felt safe or right. After several let-downs, I finally decided never to marry again and that I was done with men! I even bought myself a ruby ring and said vows with God. God became my husband. *By the way, that is an awesome way to live a single life! God is a great husband.*

However, I began to feel a tug in my heart that God wanted my children to have a dad to help raise them, and that He wanted me to be cherished by a man. I made this giant list and put it before God of everything I thought I wanted or needed in a husband. It was not very long after offering that list before God in prayer that I sensed this voice bigger than me saying, "Put that down, you do not know what is best for you."

I tore up the list. It came to me to pray just one thing: "Lord, give me a man who loves You more than he loves me." I figured if a man really loved God with his whole heart, then he would love me better than any other person could. *I highly recommend this prayer, if you are looking for a mate!* What a pay off!!!

Little did I know that David had given up on women and had decided to stay single, when God began tugging at him. Interestingly, this was happening to both of us in the very same months. We had a mutual friend who kept telling us about each other and we both turned down her offer to introduce us. Our wonderful and sneaky friend brought David to a concert that she knew I was attending. We met that night and all the princess dreams of a broken little girl began to come true.

There have been many instruments the Lord has used in my healing journey from all the abuse in my life, but by far, the greatest tool God has used in my life is my incredible husband, David.

Ours is a journey of romance and friendship that I never imagined possible. We both agree that the greatest glue in our marriage has been my past abuse. Yes, you read correctly! My past abuse has cemented our relationship into an inseparable bond. Nobody knows me or understands me better than he does. David reminds me of a skilled locksmith or a safe cracker. There seems to be no door he cannot open when it comes to working with me. He listens for the cogs turning and clicking and then blasts things wide open! He is gentle and strategic but gets me where I need to be in order to open up and receive healing. He will receive a huge crown for his patience one day, I believe.

When I had my first flashback followed by several months of severe PTSD, my David was beside me through this ordeal. He is a tender warrior who has held me through many painful memories. He was trained in inner healing specifically so that he could minister to me. He has spent countless nights after feeling prompted by the Lord to awaken me and begin ministry. As I shared earlier, I am most pliable in my sleep and my defenses are down. David learned this early on in my healing journey and he has sacrificed much sleep on my behalf.

David has learned to watch for signs or symptoms that something is stirring up in me. The Holy Spirit often prompts him or whispers trigger words into his mind. In one situation, a start of a memory was quickly dismissed because I just could not accept that the person in my memory was involved in this specific nightmarish memory! I did not mention anything to my husband. The very next day, he asked me if I knew someone by this very name! Now, it is not a common name in the first place and we did not currently know anyone by this name. David told me that he awoke and sensed God telling him to ask me about this name! This is obviously not a coincidence. Naturally, we worked through that memory and it actually opened an entire portion of my life that I had been unwilling to deal with previously.

I am a hard case. I like to be in control and I do not like to feel emotion. I spent my entire life running from pain and I learned the art of survival very well. God knew exactly who was needed in my life, a man who is submitted to the Holy Spirit and who loves greatly.

One evening I awoke to David whispering "I love you" over and over in my ear. I smiled and fell asleep only to awake a while later to him still repeating the phrase. He shared with me that the Lord had asked him to repeat, "I love you, I love you, I love you," to me ten thousand times! I do not know how many hundreds or thousands he has spoken over me thus far, but I never fail to awaken several times a month to hear these words being repeated over and over by my faithful husband.

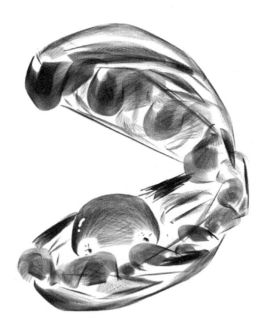

David has allowed me the privilege of ministering inner healing to his life's deepest hurts as well. We walk through these painful places together and each time we are connected even deeper. The depth of relationship when you trust someone so fully and intimately with your deepest hurts, your deepest secrets, your deepest betrayals is unfathomable! If we could only train every couple in every marriage to walk together into the dark places, what healing there could be in their relationships! Imagine the gems that could be discovered in one another.

I was once a little girl with dreams before predators nearly destroyed my hopes. The hopes and dreams died for a very long season, but God resurrected them in a wonderful human, my David. We blended our families and raised six children. David had three from his first marriage, he adopted my two children, and then we had one child together. We are now enjoying the fruit of our marriage in our children and grandchildren. We share our very passionate love for one another, and we seek our God together through every adventure that comes our way. Our mutual love and respect of one another is so evident to others that recently one of our grandsons told us that he only wants to get married if he can have a marriage like ours!

Dreams can come true, even for those of us who would have been thrown away by others. My husband took me in, dusted me off, unlocked me, and found the treasure that God knew was hidden inside. I still cannot believe I got my true knight in shining armor! Imagine the gems that can be discovered and the pearls that can be revealed in one another!

PEACE IN THE PUZZLE

There is a word that most wish to avoid when referring to nearly any victim of sexual abuse, sexual assault, or sex trafficking. Forgiveness is often considered the "F"-word to most abuse survivors. This word is a hotly debated one when working with survivors. It is the topic of forgiveness. I consider this piece of the puzzle that is our life to be central to forming a beautiful finished picture.

I have lost count of the numerous survivors who have come to me broken-hearted or feeling lost because someone told them that all they need to do is forgive and forget! Hesitancy to work with Christian ministries among those working with abuse victims is very common due to this impossible demand being placed upon the victims. Our brains were created to remember, even if the memory is stored in the subconscious. Only God has the true Divine ability to forget. "I will forgive their wickedness and will remember their sins no more" (Hebrews 8:12). While we are made in the image of our Creator, we are not able to do or be all that God is. We are not omnipotent, walking this world in unlimited power, and we certainly are not perfect.

In fact, one of our local advocacy agencies called me a few years ago and asked me if I could please come explain my beliefs on forgiveness because they were turned off by how some pastors were directing survivors to forgive, forget, bury it, and move on. Grieved by this lack of compassion or understanding, I could hardly wait to meet with this organization and give them my perspective as a Christian. Once I shared my basic tenets regarding forgiveness, they were relieved at my response and we began collaborating. I began speaking on their behalf in schools, as well. My training and beliefs in this area became so well accepted that I was able to teach on the topic of forgiveness in a humanities class at a local university for several semesters. Mind you, this is not because I changed the truth to match someone's acceptance or ability to tolerate it. I would never do that because my sincere belief is that God's ways are perfect. People just tend to misinterpret what God is actually saying in the Bible and then bend it to fit what we are comfortable with.

I can explain forgiveness in a way that is not only acceptable to any survivor but will hopefully encourage each one to walk through this process. It is unlike many things you will hear or have been taught regarding this topic. The ability to explain this in an acceptable way only can occur because it is downloaded to me by God. God still speaks to our soul and to our spirit. We have just become too busy, too impatient, and too preoccupied to take the time to listen.

Recognizing the purpose for forgiveness is vital. However, to do that, one must first weed out what forgiveness is NOT. It is not the same as reconciling. Reconciliation is an entirely different process, different definition, and certainly not recommended in trafficking. Forgiveness is also not the same as excusing. There is no excuse for the behavior of traffickers, pimps, or the tricks (clientele).

Important to know is the reality that the greatest benefactor of forgiveness is you, the person doing the forgiving. As a survivor, or for that matter anyone who needs to forgive others, it is a rare situation that the offending party will ever know they have been forgiven by you. You certainly are not going to make a phone call to the very people you have escaped from and tell them you have forgiven them! That would be incredibly dangerous and ill-advised!

The question that is probably foremost in your mind then, is why forgive at all? I cannot state it strongly enough—YOU have so much to gain by forgiving! You also have something very weighty to lose, something that will not be missed by you. As I was seeking out the idea of forgiveness and understood that as a Christian, I am commanded to forgive, I wondered why. It did not seem fair. I thought by forgiving these monsters that I would not be holding "them" accountable.

In prayer one day, God showed me a disturbing picture. I saw these balls and chains on my ankles. Each of them had the name of a rapist on them. At once I realized that I was dragging them with me where ever I went! I could not escape them. I was giving these perpetrators "permission" to come with me everywhere in my life. They were attending some of my most important and precious moments! I was dragging them along down the aisle to my wedding ceremony, into the birthing room of my babies, to birthday parties, to holidays, etc. The recognition of this made me want to immediately cut them off my ankles and out of my life forever! I was not going to give them the freedom to intrude into one more event!

It is then that I realized that God commands us to forgive because He knows we need to forgive in order to free ourselves! Additionally, it relieves us of a growing issue that will soon become bitterness. Bitterness causes many physical detriments to our bodies. The added bonus of forgiving is that it also puts us in right standing with our God.

Another incredibly important factor that I learned is that I could not forgive by minimalizing the offenses. We all do this without realizing it. When we are offended, and we decide we want to forgive the offender; we often shrink the offense to a size we can face. As an example, let me use a pizza as the full size of an offense.

Imagine that an uncle rapes his niece. The niece cares for this uncle somewhat, and especially does not want to upset the family. To deal with the situation, she begins to excuse the uncle because he was drunk. In this way, she now takes a pepperoni off the pizza. Next another excuse comes to mind that this uncle had a bad childhood, and another pepperoni comes off the pizza. Pondering the event, the victim remembers that he was watching a provocative movie beforehand, and another pepperoni is removed. Excuse after excuse, pepperoni pieces are removed and finally slices of pizza until only a small piece of pepperoni remains. Now the niece can face that smaller offense, that pepperoni-sized offense, and she chooses to forgive *that.* Only that, the watered down, excused and minimalized version of the full offense. Meanwhile, the rest of that entire pizza-sized offense remains on the inside. It is in there, festering, boiling, aching, and undealt with. The niece minimalized the offense to a size that was tolerable and much easier to forgive. Had she faced the entire pizza, which she felt too large to forgive, she could have been fully set free.

Unfortunately, we do this in many situations in life and all the while the entire offense is still lurking underneath, undealt with. Left unattended to, this hidden pizza-sized event will most likely surface one day in more extreme ways, leaving a wake of consequences behind it. In the meantime, it is also causing internal health damage. We must forgive the entire pizza to be free!

The relief that you, the forgiver, receives when you forgive the entire offense is one of the most freeing feelings you will ever experience! The balls and chains come off and you are free to dance through life without the heavy weights holding you back. The spring in your step will return!

When I pray to forgive, I use the term "release" in my prayer. In case you are uncertain how to approach this, here is an example of how I pray, "God, I choose to forgive *name* for list all offense(s). I release *name* from my anger, my hatred, my bitterness, and my revengeful emotions. Please release *name* now." I then hand them off to the Lord knowing they are His to deal with, not mine. At this point, I like to take a deep breath, blow it out, and feel the release. Sweet freedom nearly immediately comes in like a flood! Remember that forgiveness is a choice. If you choose to forgive, be careful to do this in steps. Do it when you are certain you are done hauling the offenders around with you. Should you decide to forgive before you sincerely understand the need to, you will be discontent with the outcome. You may need to forgive certain people over and over because they continue to offend you.

I pray for all who are reading this. I pray that you grasp the enormous blessing that forgiveness affords. I pray that you will be set free from those who have wounded you once and for all. There are very few things that provide as much peace to move on in your life than this process of forgiving! May you be filled to overflowing with abundant peace!

JOURNEY TO WHOLENESS

My healing journey has not ended. Facing the initial, very traumatic memories was just the beginning. I have had many other memories that would come up over the years, and they had to be dealt with as well. No more hiding from my past. God would not allow it. Anything hidden can be used on the inside to cause "infection" to set in. In each hidden thing, issues and attitudes are healed when brought into the light. It is a worthwhile journey, but most of us fight it. I have been the worst of "patients" to work with at times. I just did not want to look at one more thing.

There were so many times that something would come out in a nightmare or an outside trigger. I have lost count of the number of times that I thought, "this has got to be it! Aren't I done now?!" Yet each time I would face it head-on and push through it, the reward is priceless!

There are many who live in the false belief that you should leave this all behind and never revisit your painful past, all the while quoting scriptures out of context to verify their misconceptions. In Proverbs, it says, "Lord, search me and show me if there is ANY anxious way in me" (some versions say wicked way, but that is an incorrect interpretation of the original text). We must let God search us, allow Him to shine His light into every dark corner of our soul so that it can be replaced with His light.

This is not the same as dwelling on the past or staying in it or thriving on pity. If you are stuck there, you really need to get to some good Christ-centered inner healing or find a good trauma informed therapist! These tools are invaluable in the journey to healing from any of life's traumas and dysfunctions. It is only our pride or our fear that keeps us from receiving the healing we need. We were victims of horrendous crimes and we deserve to live a life free of victimization, even that of our own making. If we stay in self-pity, then we are allowing ourselves to continue to live as victims. I will not let those who stole from me continue to steal from me any longer! Freedom comes when we are no longer living as victims but rising as warriors. We have all picked up junk from this life and we have all believed lies about ourselves, God, others, or the world around us. Let us take back our lives. You do not need to be a survivor of sex slavery to utilize this truth.

Inner healing (healing prayer) is a magnificent, practical, and yet supernatural way to allow the Lord to get to the roots of these issues and pull them out. The most incredible part of it is that you get to "hear" what the Lord has to say about it all. God is always loving, always forgiving, always kind, and ever merciful! You will get to see a side of God that you may never have known, that has been hidden from you because of the lies and dysfunctions of the past.

God wants to be your everything! Not because He is egotistical or needy, but because He knows what YOU need. He knows that every human being needs Him, because God is truly a loving parent that is faithful, protective, understanding, and kind. In most cases, life has taught us the opposite.

I have learned to trust God when He allows something to come up. Therefore, I frequently refer to this as a journey. It is somewhere you are still going. You have not quite arrived at your destination and the journey has not been completed. I do not believe our journey in healing really ends until we are with the Lord in eternity. Only Jesus was perfected on this earth! In fact, I have been and still am being blessed by having enrolled in Rebecca Bender Initiative (RBI) Elevate Academy specifically for trafficking survivors.[14] Rebecca Bender is a survivor leader with the drive and the skills to help other survivors to jump start their healing process. This has been so beneficial that I scarcely know where to start. There truly are issues, feelings, and thoughts that are unique to having been in slavery, and it honestly takes another survivor to understand. RBI provides this and I highly recommend it to any survivor!

While on my own healing journey, I have been privileged to help countless others walk out their journeys. Each of their stories are priceless and are too numerous to count or share. This is what it is all about - sharing what we have received.

I was once asked while speaking at a local high school if I was glad to suffer the things I had to help others. I responded to this young person by telling him that I will never be able to say I am glad

---

[14] Rebecca Bender, survivor and founder of Rebecca Bender Initiative, Elevate Academy, author, speaker, trainer.

that I went through the horrendous traumas in my life. I am, however, glad that I can use those situations to help others. I hope this book serves to do that very thing.

> Experiences are not just what happen to us, they are the raw material we use in shaping our identity, our self. The person we become can think about the events that shaped us, reevaluate them, and choose how to respond to them. We are not prisoners of our past; we can retain control over how we decide to use aspects of our past in shaping who we want to be and to become.[15]

I recognize that my past has had an enormous impact on who I am. I am an overcomer and more than a survivor. Surviving that life has caused me to be more compassionate, to find joy in even the smallest things, and to do my very best not to judge others harshly. I have chosen to do all that I can to walk away a better person. Every bit of suffering that we endure in this life is an opportunity to become bitter or better. If I allow bitterness to have its way, then I allow the perpetrators in my past to continue to have a part in molding me. I choose NOT to allow them any place in my life or in further shaping me! I choose freedom!

The following is an extensive list of some of the signs and symptoms of trafficking in the Midwest/Heartland of the USA. These indicators are not limited to this area alone because ring trafficking transpires nation-wide. (This is an experiential list from my life and the lives of other survivors from rural areas whom I have personally conversed with.)

---

[15] Krystine I Batcho PhD, "What Your Oldest Memories Reveal About You." Psychology Today https://www.psychologytoday.com/us/blog/longing-nostalgia/201504/what-your-oldest-memories-reveal-about-you [06/13/2018]

- Rebellion
- Disconnection from family and/or friends
- Depression or Anxiety
- Use of drugs or alcohol – specifically to the blackout phase or to hallucinate (escaping reality)
- Insecurity or self-hatred
- Sleep issues or frequent nightmares
- Sexualized or seductive behavior or attire
- Tattoos related to trafficking (names of pimps, barcodes)
- Unexplained weight loss
- Baffling cuts, bruises, burns
- Secretive relationships or social media contacts
- Unusual interest or attention towards your child by adult(s)
- Inexplicable exhaustion
- STD's
- Frequent health issues or lowered immune system
- Sudden loss in hygiene or extreme attention to hygiene
- Difficulty making direct eye contact with others
- Uncomfortable laughter or smiles (often mistaken for insincerity)
- Deception or secrets surrounding whereabouts
- Dark circles under the eyes or unexplained bloodshot eyes
- Extreme intrigue with sex and/or pornography
- Relationships with significantly older men and/or women
- Ties to criminal elements, criminal motorcycle clubs, or street gangs (in the larger communities)

It should be noted that a single symptom does not necessarily constitute a concern that someone is being trafficked. A combination of any of these may be a danger sign and should not be disregarded.

It is my belief that if three or more of these are present without a known cause, it should warrant concern that something other than usual behavior may be involved.

If caught while a child is still young, during the grooming stage, the progression can very likely be brought to an end. However, once the programming or mind control has taken root, it will be difficult to get a child to be able to expose what is happening, yet it is not impossible! With today's resources, especially within the last decade, children are being exposed to more education regarding this issue. Educating them plays one of the biggest roles in this battle against trafficking. To educate the children, parents must be educated themselves. I pray that you do not feel overwhelmed by what you have read, rather that you will feel called to the battle either actively or on your knees (or both).

It must be mentioned that nearly anywhere in the world, the plague of familial trafficking is found operating in significant numbers and the Heartland is no exception. These families are often intertwined with rings and trade their own children between other families, pimps, and organizations. I am friends with many who have been trafficked this way. The added pain of parents, spouses, or other family members being involved is incredibly devaluing. Naturally, in these cases, it is difficult to get information from the victims as the programming is generally done on a continuous basis right in the home.

In the Midwest, it is important to be aware that there is also a great deal of trafficking at truck stops. For more information or to educate yourself on signs of this, you can request materials by visiting the site for Truckers Against Trafficking (TAT) at www.truckers againsttrafficking.org

Information like this can be overwhelming but turning a blind eye to it only increases the ability for growth of the sex slavery agenda. Now allow me to give you some more hope.

I pray right now as you are nearing completion of From Trafficked to Treasured that you will sense the tug to work on your own journey, whatever that may be. God is standing by, ever waiting to have that special time with you. Remember this truth: You do not need to walk down any healing path alone.

ALABASTER VESSEL

In my early twenties, just a brief time after leaving that life, I moved back to my home state. For the first time in my adult life, I chose a church to attend. It was a sweet little church filled with loving people and great leaders. There I learned that God is real and not just some far away being that cares little for what goes on in our lives. I learned that God speaks today to His children just as He did in the Old Testament.

There was a specific thing that was shared with me over and over by several different people. It first began in this little church and continued through the next several years. People would come up to me and say that they got a visual picture of me in their mind and "saw" me as a wine glass tipped over on the edge of a table being poured out. When I would inquire as to the meaning of this, no one had the answer. I heard this for a number of years and it caused me to be more curious each time. What did this mean?!

Then came the incident that I referenced earlier where I was going through severe flashbacks of the first gang rape. I was regularly meeting with several women in ministry. One of these women was someone I was just getting to know. Neither she nor the others knew what I was personally going through in my private life. As we came to gather one afternoon, I was prepared to ask them to pray for me regarding what I was going through and whether I should start a support group to help others as well as myself.

Before I was able to share, this wonderful woman walked in and said that she had something very specific to share with me. She said, "Kelly, I see you as a wine glass tipped over on the edge of a table being poured out." I was about to sigh and inquire as to its meaning when she continued. "And here is the meaning of this— whatever you are currently going through is the very thing God wants to use you in, He wants to pour you out so that you will help others with that which you are dealing with." Finally, I had the understanding! She then added, "This will not be the only time you are poured out; there will be other things."

Being poured out in this issue made sense of all that I had been through. When you are poured out, you literally give all that you have and allow it to splash all over those around you. It then soaks into others and they absorb what you have to offer. Of course, individuals can choose to be sponges and soak it up or to turn to stone and let it run off. It is their choice. I had a choice too. I could accept this pouring out, or I could walk away. Obviously, walking away was not my choice. It would never be my choice to do so. The voiceless ones call out to me. The wounded ones call out to me. I hear them crying and I must answer their cries.

Alabaster Vessel

A few months after starting my first support group, a young man came up to me and said he had something to share with me. He said he was new at hearing things from God, but that he had a picture in his mind where he saw me as an alabaster pitcher being poured out upon thousands and thousands! He asked if I knew what it meant. My husband was standing with me. We smiled and nodded our heads to affirm that he was indeed hearing from the same voice that had spoken to me through others many times before.

The alabaster pitcher was an upgrade and an enlargement of the previous wine glass. It solidified in me a destiny to never hold back from reaching out of my suffering to touch others. Why suffer and bury it so that it is of no value? That has never been, nor will it ever be the way I choose to live. I am a poured out one.

Additionally, I recognized the significance of alabaster. Biblically, it is an incredibly expensive commodity. A woman broke an alabaster container and poured oil on the head and feet of Jesus to prepare Him for His ultimate ministry on this earth. She was a woman who was looked down upon by those in the room because they felt she was wasting a very expensive perfume. The perfume was worth a year's wages, so they questioned why Jesus would allow her to waste such expensive perfume! They did not see what He saw in her. She washed His feet with her tears. They did not feel what He felt for her. He loved her. In their eyes, she was an unlikely minister touching the feet of the Messiah. They would have missed her significance and her value, but Jesus did not. In fact, He responded to their short sightedness by saying, "Why are you bothering this woman? She has done a beautiful thing to Me. Truly I tell you, wherever this gospel is preached throughout the world, what she has done will also be told, in memory of her" (Matthew 26:6-12).

Survivors are likened to this woman described in Luke seven. We are unlikely heroes. We are called to pour out that which was incredibly expensive to us, that which cost us greatly. Men and women who walk with reputations that some spurn; yet resisting their vile words, we can hold on to the One who values us. He will take hold of our chins and lift them up, so that our worth might be recognized. We are alabaster vessels filled to overflowing with much to pour out so that the lives of others might be saved.

Whatever your experiences in this life, may the God of all comfort speak to you about how valuable you are! In fact, you are priceless. I pray that you are assured of this truth: God will not waste your suffering.

GLOSSARY

This glossary is free to use and not bound by the copyrights of this book;
with the condition that the author and book title are cited.

Dissociation – occurs when a situation is so traumatizing that a person mentally disconnects themselves from a situation; also, when extreme emotions are compartmentalized into different locations within the subconscious mind (referred to as fragmenting).

Escort Service – hiring of a prostituted person as a "date" at parties, conventions, homes, or hotels, often for lengthy periods of time.

Flashbacks – reliving of a traumatic event where all of the senses are engaged as though one has travelled back in time and landed within the initial traumatic event.

Grooming – diverse combinations of sexual trauma often beginning with subtle touch and kindness; escalates to torture, threats, and manipulation to break down a victim to a state of compliance.

Guerilla Tactics – use of violence, force, and torture to control the victim.

Hypervigilance – a state of living in extreme response to situations causing one to be intensely sensitive to even the slightest perception of threat.

Integrate – when a person who has dissociated into parts or fragments of themselves is able to bring those compartmentalized areas of the mind into one space within the conscious mind; combining these parts into the whole or core of the person.

Pipeline – a circuit, or chain of cities or states among which prostituted people are moved through.

Ring Trafficking – criminal organizations involving several linked people in various locations that are involved in sex trafficking.

Romeo Pimp – begins relationship with an intended victim, romanticizes the relationship with gifts and compliments until they have the victim away from safety and help.

Survival Mode – a condition of going through the motions of life without feeling emotions; state which one slips into when encountering difficult situations that stir up undesirable emotions.

Squares – refers to anyone not involved in the trafficking lifestyle.

The Life/The Game – refers to living in a life surrounded, associated with, and engulfed by all the aspects of the sex industry and trafficking, especially associated with prostitution.

Trick – a person paying for the act of prostitution.

Trigger – outside stimulation that reminds a person of another similar negative time, place, or event; generally involving one or more of a person's senses causing negative reactions.

Turned Out – to be forced into active prostitution, generally refers to one being newly involved with the intent of forced continuation.

Made in the USA
Middletown, DE
11 January 2019